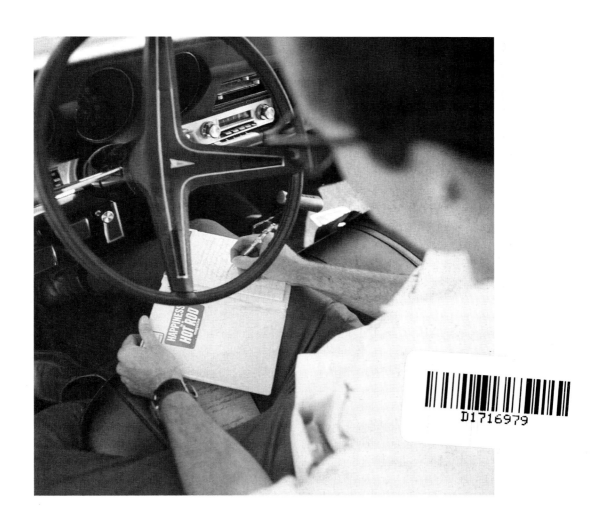

MUSCLE CAR
FILES

Selected Road Tests 1964–1971

From the editors of *Hot Rod* Magazine

MOTORBOOKS
INTERNATIONAL

This edition first published in 2003 by Motorbooks International, an imprint of
MBI Publishing Company, Galtier Plaza, Suite 200, 380 Jackson Street, St. Paul, MN
55101-3885 USA

Motorbooks International titles are also available at discounts in bulk quantity for
industrial or sales-promotional use. For details write to Special Sales Manager at
Motorbooks International Wholesalers & Distributors, Galtier Plaza, Suite 200,
380 Jackson Street, St. Paul, MN 55101-3885 USA.

ISBN 0-7603-1647-3

On the front cover: After evaluating the 1971 Plymouth Barracuda, *Hot Rod* deemed
the car a *super* supercar.

On the frontispiece: A *Hot Rod* car tester takes notes on his evaluation of Pontiac's
GTO Judge.

On the title page: Two 1970 Firebirds head down the highway during a road test.

On the back cover: While those who evaluated the 1969 GTO Judge found its
performance a bit lacking when compared to previous GTO tests, they were not
disappointed with the results: "Any time a supercar in ultra-stock form even breaks into
the 14-second region, we're happy."

Edited by Leah Noel
Designed by Kou Lor

Printed in the United States of America

CONTENTS

INTRODUCTION

David Freiburger,
editor in chief of *Hot Rod* Magazine

The early years of the new millennium brought a new catch phrase to describe the freshest segment of hot rodding: sport compact cars. The kids who've been hopping up Datsun B210s and Mazda RX7s since the '80s are now the icons of cool. Sport compacts have their own drag racing series, the OE manufacturers are falling all over themselves to produce new performance models, the aftermarket is grappling for a share of the business, and the traditional hot rodders are looking on with distain.

We're sure you've seen it. And whether you're too young to have lived it or too old to recall it, the excitement surrounding today's scene is exactly what was going down in the early '60s; back then, American muscle cars were the rage. An inkling of what was to come was Chevy's 1958 Tri-Power 348s or maybe Ford's 360 horsepower, 352-ci FE engine package in '60, but by the time the '62 Mopars with the 413-ci Max Wedge engines were released, the true muscle car had been defined: big power, lightweight, V-8 powered, and rowdy. Some argue that the real first muscle car was the '64 GTO, and others define the '68 Road Runner as the icon of the era.

Regardless, by the time Lyndon Johnson assumed office, muscle cars were booming. The National Hot Rod Association (NHRA) adopted the Super Stock class to support Detroit's efforts, new performance models were released in legion numbers from every manufacturer, and many of the aftermarket companies we know today were making their names known on the drag strips and streets of the nation. Cruise scenes such as Woodward Avenue in Detroit and Van Nuys Boulevard in Los Angeles became known nationally. Glorified in TV shows, movies, and song, muscle cars had become pop culture. And predictably, the traditional hot rodders of the time—the guys who'd run flathead roadsters on the dry lakes since before World War II—looked at it all with certain distain.

But they still read about it all in *Hot Rod*, as the magazine was bursting in each issue with news on all the factory horsepower, from drag strip coverage and inside news from Detroit to frequent road tests of the latest iron. You could read about the proven performance of a 425-horsepower Hemi in *Hot Rod* on one day, then walk to the Plymouth dealer and buy one the next day. We can't bring back Hemi Cudas on the showroom floor, but we can give you a glimpse of what it was like in the heyday as we present a collection of *Hot Rod* Magazine's road tests from 1964 to 1971. Sadly, only two of the automotive nameplates reviewed in this book survive today: the legendary Pontiac GTO, re-introduced after a 30-year absence, and Ford's popular favorite, the Mustang. It makes us wonder, if there were still muscle cars today, would there be a sport compact car trend?

INTRODUCTION   7

STUDEBAKER LARK WITH R-3 PERFORMANCE

RAY BROCK
Hot Rod, January 1964

A new image for Studebaker is being established in the field of performance with custom-built Avanti power and chassis options now available in the Lark

Studebaker has been in the business of building transportation vehicles for quite a few years now and has gone through many phases. They started way back in the days before the automobile was invented with covered wagons rolling off the assembly lines in South Bend, Indiana. After the switch to horsepower derived from gasoline instead of hay, Studebaker became one of the automobile pioneers.

Look through records of early Indianapolis 500-mile races and you'll see where Studebakers were among the faster cars on the track. Top drivers of the era chose Stude, and the car had quite a performance reputation. Just prior to World War II, one of the hottest cars on American roads was the Studebaker President, a big, straight-eight powered car that had pretty sneaky body lines for its day and could really cover ground.

Then right after the war, there was the double-ender Stude. Remember that one? Everybody else in the automobile business had dusted off their pre-war dies and with a few trim changes, started making the same cars they'd had back in 1942, but not Studebaker. The automaker brought out a brand-new body style with a rounded off front and rear that sold like hotcakes. Of course there had been no cars available to civilians since late 1941 and any automobile sold like hotcakes. Some practical jokers who bought Studes actually went so far as to put signs denoting "front" and "rear" on their cars so pedestrians would know whether these models were coming or going.

By the late 1940s and early 1950s, Detroit production had caught up with consumer demands and competition between manufacturers became torrid, so new styles and mechanical features became big selling points. Studebaker really startled the industry in 1953 when the company introduced the Loewey-designed, way-out model, which many automotive buffs still claim to be the slipperiest car ever built. Styling changes were minor during the next few years, but Studebaker became the economy champ of the era with a thrifty little six, coupled to an overdrive transmission and the wind-cheating shape.

The short overhang and excellent ground clearance of the Lark make the car ideal for rutted, rocky country roads.

Through the late '50s and early '60s, though, Studebaker did not have anything particularly exciting to talk about. The larger, wealthier companies in Detroit brought out new styles more often than Studebaker could afford to match. New engines, new models, big advertising budgets—Stude couldn't keep up with the pace and sales started slipping. Studebakers weren't fast, they weren't stylish, and compared to some of the new small-engine compacts on the road, they weren't particularly economical. There was no longer an image connected with the name Studebaker.

For the past couple of years, though, things have been happening in South Bend to restore image to Studebaker. Management changes were made and a new, young president named Sherwood Egbert took over reins of the corporation. Diversification into new fields—chemicals, appliances, tractors, space technology—13 divisions in all, have placed the corporation on sound footing, and now the big push is on to bring the automotive division back onto the black side of the ledger. The first tipoff on things to come was the mid-year introduction of the Avanti in 1962. It was a styling sensation, but Avanti hit production snags that prevented dealers from making immediate deliveries, so it got off to a very slow start sales-wise.

The Avanti did a lot for Studebaker's styling image, though, and management soon followed up this accomplishment with a performance program that made enthusiasts take note. One of the acquisitions during Studebaker's diversification program was Paxton

An R-3 installation uses a cast-aluminum air box enclosure for the four-barrel carburetor. The alternator and transistor ignition are by Prestolite; the supercharger is Paxton.

Products, a supercharger manufacturer in Santa Monica, California. Studebaker also acquired the talents of Andy, Joe, and Vince Granatelli, a brother team with considerable experience in the field of performance. Their first job was to go to work on the Studebaker V-8 and see what could be done to increase its power and reliability.

By late 1962, Paxton-blown Avantis had established a large number of national and international speed records on the Bonneville Salt Flats under supervision of the U.S. Auto Club. Speeds as high as 175-plus were registered in the trim Avanti, and with high-performance engines, Hawk and Lark bodies were clocked above 140 and 130, respectively. The performance push was on and it is still going strong right now.

There were many items introduced on the Avanti that management felt would appeal to potential customers in the Hawk and Lark lineup of automobiles and, although some were offered in 1963, the '64 model year is the year that customers are really being encouraged to "build a car to meet their needs." Every engine, transmission, chassis, and brake feature that is standard or optional on the Avanti is now available in both the Hawk and Lark lines. When Studebaker's West Coast public relations representative gave us this information last summer, we conceived plans for a car we felt should really be tested by *Hot Rod*.

We had already tested the Avanti R-2 and R-3 models and had been quite impressed, but for an encore we had something different in mind. Sneak views of the '64 Lark line and dimensions of the cars made us decide that the Lark might be just the car to make an impression at the drag strip. Our PR contact agreed and said that he'd order a Lark to our specifications, which we could use as a magazine project in drag racing with perhaps competition in NHRA's Winternationals as the final segment of the test.

The car we ordered was a 1964 Lark Daytona two-door hardtop equipped with R-3 engine, four-speed transmission, Twin-Traction limited-slip differential, heavy-duty suspension, disc front brakes with power assist, power steering, Halibrand 15-inch magnesium wheels, bucket seat interior, radio, and heater. Sounds sort of hard to believe all this could be wrapped up in one package, doesn't it?

The Daytona Lark is only 190 inches in overall length, or just under 16 feet. Wheelbase is only 109 inches, almost identical to that used by Corvair and Falcon. Tread both front and rear is within a fraction of 57 inches. Car width is an even six feet and height is just under 55 inches.

This is a "compact car" in length, wheelbase, and appearance but not in interior space or power teams. Standard production Lark Daytona models are equipped with a two-barrel

Prior to high speed runs at Bonneville, the Lark timing was checked by Prestolite representatives. Sears Allstate Bonneville style tires were used for high-speed safety. Sears tires were used on all Studebakers during record runs.

259-inch V-8 engine rated at 180 horsepower, but engine options that have been part of the Studebaker lineup for years include a four-barrel version of the 259 with 195 horsepower rating, a two-barrel 289-inch V-8 rated 210 horsepower and a four-barrel 289 with a 225 horsepower tag.

Prior to Avanti introduction and the "R-series" engines, the 225 horsepower model was the top of the list for Studebaker, but now performance is all-important and Stude is offering some of the healthiest V-8s in the industry, inch-for-inch.

R-1 is the standard engine for the Avanti. It has the same 289-inch displacement as the 225-horsepower model but has more compression (10.25 versus 8.5) and a larger four-barrel carburetor. The R-1 is rated 240 horsepower.

Next on the optional engine list is the R-2 and this one gets a good boost in performance from a centrifugal blower manufactured by Paxton Division of Studebaker. It has 289 ci, only 9:1 compression, and a single four-barrel carburetor, but that supercharger that has a designed delivery of approximately six pounds per square inch gage gives the R-2 a horse-per-inch, 289 horsepower.

R-3 engine option is the next one on the list and this is the top of the power ladder. These R-3 engines are meticulously assembled at Paxton Products, then sent back to South

The heavy-duty suspension package includes a stabilizer bar linked between rear wheels. Note the finned drum.

Bend where they join the assembly line to fill dealer orders. The R-3 has 304.5 ci, 9.6:1 compression, a hotter camshaft than the R-2, cylinder heads with larger valves and ports, much more exact manufacturing tolerances, and the Paxton supercharger. Reluctant to place an exact power rating on its performance engines, Studebaker rates the R-3 at 335 horsepower, but to date has not advertised this figure.

An R-4 option is also available and this, too, is a hand-built engine by the Paxton Division that is then delivered to South Bend. The R-4, although latest in the R-series, does not have the advantages of forced air induction from a blower but is equipped with dual four-barrel carburetion. Most of the components used in the R-4, heads with large ports and valves, camshaft, clearances, etc., are the same as the R-3 but with carburetion instead of a supercharger. The power rating drops to 280 horsepower.

Getting back to the R-3, which is the engine we chose for our test Lark; this is a very hot item although unbelievably smooth for everyday use. Paxton receives finished, bare cylinder blocks from Studebaker's engine plant and then starts the special assembly. First, each block is carefully checked and machined if necessary to give cylinder decks exactly parallel to the crankshaft, square to the bores, and the proper height from crank on either side. Next, each cylinder is individually bored .093-inch over the 289 bore size to 3 21/32-inch and the top edges of these bores chamfered to match cylinder head combustion chambers and provide valve clearance. Finally, before engine assembly starts, the completed block is dye-checked to make sure it is perfect.

The crankshaft used in the R-3 is the same forged steel crank used in all 289-inch engines but with extra bearing clearances. With the 3 5/8-inch stroke and the extra 3/32-inch bore, the R-3 has a final displacement of 304.5 ci, or 5 liters, and this places the engine right at the top limit of National and International Class C displacement.

Bearings used in the assembly of the R-3 are heavy-duty and of either aluminum or copper-lead composition. Clearances average .001-.002 more than standard assembly procedures throughout the engine. Pistons are made to Stude specifications by Forgedtrue.

Cylinder heads used with the R-3 engines have larger ports than standard 289s and chambers are fully machined to give exact, equal chamber volumes. Large, 1 7/8-inch intake valves and 1 5/8-inch exhaust valves are fitted to the heads. Most R-3 engines are equipped with single valve springs, but inner springs are also available to match an extra high-performance camshaft designed for all-out racing.

The standard R-3 camshaft is relatively mild for a high-performance engine when compared to those used in the hot 427-inch V-8s being built nowadays. It has 276-degree duration for both intake and exhaust and 48-degree valve overlap. This "mild" timing is the reason the R-3 engine idles so smoothly and points out one of the beautiful aspects of supercharging an engine; wild cam timing is not needed to fill the cylinder since extra pressure is available to do the job. Stude's part number for the 276-degree cam is 1558819. For those interested in the hottest cam, a 288-degree version (part No. 1560816) can be ordered and this one has 56-degree overlap, still mild by today's standards. The latter camshaft requires optional inner valve springs in addition to the standard outers.

Stude's V-8 is one of the few engines around today that uses timing gears instead of sprockets and timing chains. Gears are stronger, more precise, and wear less than chains, but they are also more expensive. Standard Stude V-8s use a cast-iron crank gear and fiber cam gear, but for the R-3 engine the cam is fitted with a stronger, aluminum gear.

Without going into every detail of the R-3 engine buildup, we can vouch for the exacting procedure used in its assembly, having witnessed most of the operations. After R-3 engines are complete, Paxton places each one on a dynamometer. They go through a special break-in cycle involving several different rpm ranges, water temperatures, and oil changes. Then cylinder heads are re-torqued, valve lash is reset, and the engine is timed for maximum output. The final test in this three-hour cycle is to make sure each R-3 engine equals or exceeds the 335 horsepower rating.

Only after all of the above steps are taken is the R-3 engine ready for Studebaker. It is strapped to a skid, shipped to South Bend, and ready to run full throttle the minute the completed car drives off the assembly line.

Prestolite's transistor ignition is standard equipment with the transistor pack and diode heat sink mounted just behind the grille in the cool airstream. The alternator used by Studebaker is also made by Prestolite. An air cleaner arrangement on our test car that was prototype, but is reportedly scheduled for production, has the cleaner housing recessed in the right front fender well and a sheet metal scoop to pick up cool air behind the grille.

Extra options for R-3 buyers who intend to race their car exclusively include an extra-capacity oil sump with electric recirculating pump for the blower and a high-capacity

12-pound electric fuel pump to ensure adequate supply to the carburetor. A fuel pressure regulator in the line prevents too much pressure to the carb float bowls.

We could fill several pages with copy about the R-3 engine, but we won't. It has a lot of parts and pieces found only on a supercharged engine. The Paxton blower is driven by dual V-belts tensioned by a spring-loaded idler. Pressure output varies slightly from engine to engine, but at the recommended shift point of 5,500 rpm, ours registered six pounds at the aluminum air box, which enclosed the Carter four-barrel. Paxton recommends a 5,800 red line speed on the R-3 with single valve springs, and at this engine speed our blower gage registered eight pounds. With a fixed engine-to-blower ratio, pressure will increase with engine speed, and when the engine speed goes over the 5,000 mark, pressure goes up in a hurry.

The Lark's chassis is basically the same as that used for the Avanti, and with heavy-duty suspension components, a short wheelbase, and an abundance of power, the Lark was very "quick" on corners, although with the heavier, steel body, it is not quite on a par with the Avanti.

Suspension layout is similar to that used by many American automobiles with coil springs and unequal-length A-arms up front and semi-elliptical leaf springs at the rear. The heavy-duty chassis package with which our car was equipped included front coil springs with 15 percent higher rate and an extra leaf in the rear springs to increase their rate 15 percent.

A front stabilizer bar is standard equipment on all Larks, but in addition, a rear stabilizer bar is added in the heavy-duty package. Traction bars from brackets on top of the rear axle housing, forward to the frame rails in front of each rear wheel, are also included in the heavy-duty kit. They prevent acceleration "squat" and wheel hop, as well as "dive" on stops. Also included in the chassis package are heavy-duty shock absorbers on all four corners.

The optional magnesium wheels are made by Halibrand, and although simulated knock-offs, they bolt right to the conventional lug bolt pattern. They are 15-inchers and have six-inch rim width. The knock-off nut is a slip-fit into the wheel's center bore and is held in position by a large O-ring instead of set screws. This permits easy removal or rotation to fit a wrench on the lug nuts.

Optional brakes were borrowed from the Avanti with Bendix discs on the front, with finned cast-iron drums at the rear. The Bendix units are made under license to Dunlop with cast-iron, 11 1/2-inch diameter discs attached to the front hubs. A cast-iron caliper is bracketed to the spindle and straddles the disc with hydraulic cylinders forcing two-inch square lining segments against each side of the disc. This type of brake is extremely good, makes straight-line stops, has excellent fade-resistance, and is unaffected by dirt or moisture. It does require higher hydraulic line pressure, however, since the units are not self-energizing. To produce this extra line pressure, a vacuum-assisted power brake unit is part of the disc brake package.

Rear brakes are conventional shoe type with 11-inch cast-iron drums finned for rapid heat dissipation. Shoe width is two inches. To be compatible with the disc front brakes and high line pressure used, a small rear wheel cylinder is used to actuate the rear shoes. Parking cables are also fitted to the rear brakes.

Taking time out from the mechanical description of the Lark, we have to interject the comment that these brakes are tops in all ways when it comes to halting a car. Pedal "feel" is good, there is no noise sometimes associated with disc brakes, there is never "swerve" on sudden application, and the price of less than $100, including power assist, is quite reasonable.

R-3 engines can be ordered with either a four-speed transmission or Stude's Warner-built automatic transmission. From past experience with an R-3 Avanti and automatic, we can verify that the two units go together quite well, but with an engine that gets its performance upstairs when the blower boost comes on, a four-speed is a much more practical selection.

Two sets of ratios are available in the Borg-Warner four-speeds: 2.54, 1.89, 1.51, and 1:1 for the standard gearbox and an optional gear set of 2.20, 1.66, 1.31, and 1:1. Obviously, with a low numerical rear-axle ratio, the set with 2.54 low is best for all-around use. With a high numerical axle, such as for drag racing, the 2.20-low is best. Our Lark was equipped with 2.20s.

Optional Halibrand magnesium wheels fit the standard lug pattern. Knock-offs are held in bore with an O-ring.

Rear-axle ratios for R-3–equipped cars run from 2.87 to 4.89 with all ratios considered optional and none listed as standard. In other words, buyers of Studebaker cars who choose the R-3 option may also choose the ratio they want and have it factory-installed. The Spicer-type rear axle, which does not have a removable center section, discourages frequent gear changes so a customer should be sure of what he wants when he orders a hot Stude. All ratios are available with optional Twin-Traction limited-slip differential.

While Studebaker was conducting its series of record-breaking runs at Bonneville last October, Managing Editor Dick Wells took our test Lark to the salt flats and joined the factory team for a day with some high-speed runs. The Lark was equipped with 3.31 rear-axle ratio, outfitted with a set of Sears Allstate Bonneville high speed tires, fitted with a new set of Champion spark plugs, and an open exhaust replaced the mufflers.

With the added comfort of a roll bar installation by Paxton Division, Dick "cruised" through the USAC timing lights at a speed of 149.98 miles per hour for the flying mile and in the last section, where the USAC also had kilometer traps set up, was clocked at 150.04 miles per hour. Dick said the ride was smooth as silk with the tach registering just 6,000 rpm and blower boost at six pounds. At sea level, blower boost between 5,800 and 6,000 would have been approximately eight pounds but the 4,300-foot elevation of the salt flats cuts pressure.

Although the ultimate plans for our test Lark called for extensive drag strip participation, it takes a lot of time to be competitive in class. So instead of installing a 4.55 or 4.89 axle ratio after the Bonneville runs, we decided to use "street" gearing and try the Lark on all types of terrain and under many conditions before we went draggin' for keeps. The ratio installed in the Lark was 3.73:1 with Twin-Traction.

As we mentioned earlier, the R-3 powerplant is surprisingly docile and we used it for transportation through Los Angeles traffic. When first delivered, the R-3 straight-through, glass-pack mufflers were too loud for comfort and we spent most of the first day with one eye on the rearview mirror anticipating a motorcycle with a red light. Fortunately, we didn't pick up a citation before we turned the car back to Paxton for a conventional dual-exhaust system, which quieted the monster. In later drag strip tests, the car will be equipped with header outlets that can be uncapped for maximum noise and performance.

In the mountains north of the Los Angeles basin, we found the blown Lark to be quite adaptable to both the road and altitude. Handling was very good on the roads we chose with twisting switchback turns. The short wheelbase and power made the Lark a hard package to match. We encountered altitudes well above 6,000 feet and the engine ran flawlessly. This is because the enclosed carburetor compensates for altitude changes. As the car is driven to higher elevations, blower boost is less for a given rpm, and pressure on the float bowls is also lessened, causing decreased fuel flow through the jets.

We found a home for the Lark on rutted dirt roads through some of the foothill sections of the mountains. With a minimum of body overhang, front and rear, plus a short wheelbase, 15-inch wheels, and excellent ground clearance beneath the car, we found the Lark to be the best American-produced sedan we've tried in years on less-than-ideal roads. Ruts, rocks, and washout sections that would have left the normal sedan high and dry didn't even phase the Lark.

Acceleration tests on a lonely stretch of level road proved the R-3 Lark had plenty of get up and go, even with the 3.73 rear-axle ratio and large diameter tires. The Lark had been equipped with tires of butyl compound to give best tractive qualities, but even so we had to be careful with starts on clean, dry asphalt to prevent excessive wheelspin. Zero to 60 miles per hour checks averaged right around six seconds flat, but we had to shift from first to second at about 53 miles per hour to keep from exceeding the 5,500 rpm shift speed recommended by Paxton, and wheelspin on the 1-2 shift made the speedometer needle jump so that it was difficult to guess just where it indicated 60 miles per hour. Zero to 80 speeds were just about 10 seconds flat, and with a steadier speedometer at this speed, we were reasonably accurate.

The only good place to check the Lark for acceleration performance, however, is the drag strip and that's where we intend to put the car to work. There's only one problem here, however, and it is all based on Stude's refusal to advertise power ratings of its R-series engines. The NHRA requires an advertised rating to compute against car weight for classification in Stock classes. Stude has in the past used the statement that these engines produce "more than enough power to suit the needs of the driver." This still does not tell how many pounds of Avanti or Lark there are per horse, so as we go to press, the NHRA will not classify the cars "stock." They have to compete in Gas Supercharged class.

The horsepower figures we gave when discussing the high-performance engines, 240 for R-1, 289 for R-2, 335 for R-3, and 280 for R-4, were obtained by telephone conversation and not from printed fact sheets. Studebaker has refused to publish these ratings, and it is suspected that even these were derived only after consulting NHRA's rule book and weight chart. The thing that makes these cars hard to classify even if advertised ratings were published is the fact that blower pressure cannot be checked.

With 3.73 rear-axle ratio and limited-slip differential, the test Lark proved to have abundance of traction, even on very steep dirt roads. It climbed hills like a goat.

Blower boost means power, and the more the boost, the more an engine will deliver, within other design limits of the engine. Just how easy it is for an owner to tamper with blower output through internal modifications, or ratio changes, we don't know, but it would appear that a sharp owner could "tune" quite a few more horses out of the blower. Agreed, the engine or blower might be overstressed and scatter, but it also might go like a bomb for a while.

So, like we said, we plan to do some dragging with this Lark. We don't know what class we'll be in, but we hope that Studebaker files the necessary classification papers so we can run in a Stock class. The car feels quite impressive, really starts to move above 3,000 rpm, and it would be a shame not to have a shot at some trophies.

We'll keep you informed as to how we make out in later issues.

OLDS 442

ERIC DAHLQUIST
Hot Rod, March 1965

Probably unlike any Olds you've ever handled; a firm ride and super control are enhanced with a 400-ci V-8 and silky-smooth four-speed

At one time, roughly about a decade and a half ago, the name Oldsmobile struck awe into the hearts of most would-be stock car drag artists and captured the imagination of the young motoring American as one of the fastest accelerating stockers ever produced. And even as organized quarter-mile racing got its first foothold, Oldsmobile dominated the stock drag classes and a few others as well. It wasn't hard to figure out why. The Olds of the early 1950s had a large (for the time) 303-ci mill stuffed into a reasonably light body. The icing on the cake was that everything in the drive train and, most significant, the engine itself was big and beefy, well able to withhold the onslaught of continual abuse.

Each autumn, at the time of new car announcements and before the phenomenon of half and fourth-year models, almost as if by magic the Oldsmobile engineering crew pulled a yet more rapid Rocket out of the hat. Nineteen fifty-five looked like another sure bet, but the lighter, high-winding little Chevy left them at the gate and, except for a last gasp with the J-2 in '57, Olds faded into the relative obscurity of the medium-price range.

Being old enough to recall the bygone glory days of Olds, and armed with a knowledge that the Rockets had emerged from the immediate uncertain post-war era as the torch bearer of experimentation and innovation, we anticipated with hopeful expectation a long road test session with the division's hottest new number: the 442. On this particular evaluation we really lucked out, as the saying goes, because GM had invited us to a series of demonstrations at its Mesa, Arizona, proving grounds, so we decided to utilize the trip to wring out the new Olds as well. A bit more savor was added to the plot when it was revealed that we would be given an opportunity to run the car on GM's test track. In light of all this, it seemed that we would enjoy all the time necessary to learn if the 442 lived up to its press release of being designed to embody "outstanding dimensions of performance, responsiveness, handling, and road sense."

During testing, the 442 felt steady at an indicated 90 miles per hour.

When we picked up the car the weekend before leaving on the Arizona trip, barely 120 miles were registered on the odometer, so, for all intents and purposes, it was a new machine. This particular model was the F-85 Club Coupe equipped with every high-performance option available, as well as an eye-catching coat of cream lacquer that was set off admirably by a tasteful amount of chromework. Fastened to the bow, stern, port, and starboard sides of the coupe were the 442 emblems that, in order, this year indicate 400 horsepower, a four-barrel carburetor, and dual exhaust. If you didn't know already, last season the numerical designation represented a four-barrel carburetor, four-on-the-floor, and dual exhaust, but the old order has changed to something a little hairier. Although we're getting a bit ahead of the narration, it would do well for those who tempt fate at the lights to remember this insignia to avoid future competitive embarrassment. Even the grille on this job has been redone slightly for the high-performance look; we think it is smart looking.

The spec sheet we received with the car enumerated the salient aspects of the 442 as well as a complete breakdown of differences between it and the stock Cutlass model. The engine is not a beefed-up version of last season's 330-ci unit; but rather an under-bored variation of the all-new Stage II, 425-inch Rocket, a report of which appeared in the November 1964 issue of *Hot Rod*. With a 4-inch bore and 3.975-inch stroke, this is barely an over-square design that belts out lots of torque for which Oldsmobiles have been

This particular model, the F-85 Club Coupe, came equipped with every high-performance option available, as well as an eye-catching coat of cream lacquer that was set off admirably by a tasteful amount of chromework.

famous for years—in this case, about 440 pounds per foot, at 3,200 rpm. Maximum brake horsepower has been pegged at 345 with moderate 10.2:1 compression ratio and the 4CG Rochester four-holer that enthusiasts will readily recognize as the carburetor used on popular Olds models of the past, though it has received considerable updating. An identical pot is employed in the smaller Cutlass engines, but for the 442 the primary throttle bore has been opened up an eighth-inch to 1 9/16-inch, and the secondary jets reamed .003-inch. In addition, a less restrictive ball-type fuel inlet valve has replaced the normal needle. All the carburetor modifications wouldn't be particularly significant if the fuel couldn't get to its destination in proper quantity, so a greater capacity, high-dome fuel pump has been fitted, in conjunction with a 3/8-inch outside diameter gas line instead of the usual 5/16-incher.

Roger Huntington has already given *Hot Rod*'s readers a thorough rundown on the 425 last year, and this smaller model doesn't deviate from it, except, of course, for 25 fewer cubes. Items such as a forged steel crankshaft and connecting rods, light, stamped steel rocker arms with tubular pushrods, plus those two-inch intake and 1.625-inch exhaust valves all contribute to vigorous and long-lasting health.

As backup systems for the engine, there are some well-thought-out package parts that are usually overlooked in combos like this, despite the fact they are sorely needed in most cases. One item that few people pay much attention to is the radiator, and here Olds engineers have substituted a heavy-duty job that was designed for lots of abuse. The second area, no less important and just as frequently forgotten, is the electrical system. Here a generous 70-ampere-hour battery has been provided and, coupled with the alternator, it should provide the owner with above-average longevity in almost any desired use. Modern engineering has all but eliminated the annoying engine-produced vibrations but, at the same time, the softness of the mounts normally leaves a little to be desired where constant acceleration and shifting place extra strains that can cause them to become unglued periodically. In this Rocket, they have substituted a sturdier set incorporating stops to control engine roll and, though we can't say how much the vibration frequency was elevated, if at all, engine movement was noticeably subdued. Finally, since logic tells us that the driveline is bound to suffer commensurately with severe usage, the standard driveshaft has been replaced with a new one, the design of which is such that it reduces high-speed vibrations to a minimum.

The remainder of the options reads like a road tester's dream of a decade ago come true: 50 percent higher wheel rate for the front and rear coil springs; firmer shocks to control high- and low-frequency ranges; fat front and rear stabilizer bars, about one-inch thick, to retard roll and sway; reinforced rear lower control arms with appropriate, higher rate bushings; and Red Line Royal "tiger paws" premium nylon tires on six-inch rims, an inch wider than stock, for sustained high-speed operation. They're all here, and more.

Even the frame got into the act on this car, being of more rugged design than the ordinary perimeter jobs found under the stock Cutlasses and F-85s. This addition is identical to the extra strength units law enforcement agencies demand under their specials to increase handling stability under adverse conditions.

Also in the police package vein are the 442s brakes that provide 156.3 inches of swept area. This figure is divided between front and rear so that the former, where the greatest amount of strain is, due to weight transfer in stopping, has a bit more material to cope with the extra exertion. The fact that Olds stuck to the Bendix duo-servos in the face of the current trend to disc brakes indicates the manufacturer's faith in the capability of the bigger binders.

And, while we wax on enthusiastically, in light of these things, the transmission selections are not to be found wanting, either. Standard on the 442 is the same three-on-the-column box normally found behind the big 425-inch engine. Ratios for this column shifter are: 1st, 2.59; 2nd, 1.60; 3rd, 1.00. Besides this, a three-on-the-floor all-synchro trans, replete with Hurst shifter, will come on with a little different spread of ratios: 1st, 2.42; 2nd, 1.61; 3rd, 1.00. Still another stick is the new-last-season Muncie close-ratio four-speed that is offered with or without between-the-buckets console, depending on body model. This is the box that was in the car we tested and the ratios are as follows: 1st, 2.56; 2nd, 1.91; 3rd, 1.48; 4th, 1.00. Clutch action for all the manuals is an extra-duty 11-inch assembly that should display excellent wear qualities even with abuse.

For those who desire to just stab and steer, a two-speed automatic torque converter transmission may be bought also. Olds Engineering stayed with the two-speed instead of three because it felt the variable stator arrangement offered equal performance to the three-speed. To keep things working in good shape, plates have been added to the forward and reverse clutches, while the shift point into drive was raised to 5,000 rpm. With the automatic, the standard rear-end ratio is 3.23:1, so this combo is apt to get down the road in very short order.

As soon as we cleared the Olds garage and had an opportunity to run through the gears, even in subdued fashion, it was immediately apparent that the car was long-winded. Our particular machine was outfitted with the 3.55:1 ratio in the center section and, even in city traffic, this choice appeared well suited to its task. Since the automatic job comes with a higher 3.23 ratio, we immediately set to wondering if the higher-geared rear end would combine with the stick setup. Or, how to go fast without really trying.

The weekend trial revealed no malfunctions so, with *Hot Rod* magazine photographer Eric Rickman aboard, we headed out the pike for the freeway, the California border, miles of Arizona desert, and ultimately the GM proving grounds in Mesa. It didn't take long to realize that even with the engine only partially loosened up the 442 was a "runner" with a capital R. Charging along at a posted 65, a light nudge on the go pedal would bring the speedo needle over 80 in short order. When we tanked up the first time at Indio, California, a quick division of gallons into miles disclosed that the car was covering about 12 miles on each gallon of gasoline. Even though this figure is nothing to write home about, the odometer showed a total mileage of still under 250, so we anticipated better averages later as break-in progressed, and we weren't to be disappointed.

At Indio we turned off on Routes 60-70 that streak out across the desert to Blythe, California, crossing into Arizona and beyond. In this neck of the woods—and we use the term loosely, for this is true desert country—the best method of getting territory put behind is to bear down on the accelerator, and this is just what we did. The highways in this part of the land are little affected by weather as far as smoothness goes, but at 80 even the smallest knoll may cause trouble for the unwary driver, so we were on our toes. High-speed touring was the order of the day and we mean a day at a time. The engine was running like a well-oiled sewing machine and, although no tach was provided, despite the fact that on such a machine it's a welcome adjunct, one could feel that it was loafing.

Passing was at no time a problem and all that was required to get around even the most persistent drivers was to get the secondaries open in that big Rochester, at which time it delivered a sensation akin to the kick-down in an automatic or overdrive. Acceleration at lower speeds could not be classed as pokey by any means, but in some conditions in mid-range it felt as if the fuel supply was running a trifle lean. And, later on, upon removal of the carburetor top, we did discover that the floats were set too low, so this probably accounted for it.

With the border inspection well behind, the next stop for gas was at Salome, and we were pleasantly surprised to learn that the miles per gallon had jumped to 15.5. Another thing we noticed was the interest shown, not only by fellow travelers, but mainly by the service station attendants who never failed to barrage us with questions and thereby attract a few additional bystanders. By this time we were both well aware of the comfort of the adjustable-pitch steering wheel, which reduced driving fatigue to a minimum. By pulling back on a stubby lever fastened just below the turn signal indicator arm, the wheel could be tilted down to a near-vertical position or elevated to a flatter truck-like angle. I have always appreciated the inclination of various sports car wheels but have nearly always been forced to resort to some form of physical contortion for entrance and exit due to the lowness of the wheel.

We arrived in Phoenix the night before the GM demonstration, so we decided to get some idea of the countryside, which wound up including a 10-mile jaunt down what may be best described as an undulating desert dirt road that embodied about as many bumps, curves, and just plain dust as you are likely to encounter anywhere in the country. GM literature had mentioned in passing that it also utilized many public side roads in the test programs because these little-traveled byways provide a severe trial for all components,

Constriction in the tailpipe is used to subdue the generous sound emitted by a resonatorless system.

and after our ordeal, we knew why. Yet, despite these rough conditions, the Olds showed an abundance of class in all situations. On the hump-backed surfaces, the combination of stiff shocking and firmer-than-normal springing really did the job in enabling the driver to retain control. Sweeping around the gravel turns at speed brought to light another of the 442s fortes—excellent handling. It was a simple matter to set up for a turn in fine dirt-track fashion and then power around, keeping the rear end hung out while at the same time safely avoiding an excursion into the boondocks.

At the proving grounds the next day, part of the program was devoted to allowing various members of the motoring press to make a few hot laps on the test track and the quarter-mile as well. The first attempt on the quarter-mile resulted in a 16.1-second elapsed time, with two observers aboard and a lot of wheelspin. Second time out, minus one 200-pounder and a little of the burnt rubber, we registered a 15.1-second elapsed time, dusting a 421-powered member of the GM "hot medium" family in the process. Immediately the wheels began turning in our minds as to just how this "baby" would run set up along drag competition lines. As for top speed, just the way the test car was equipped, only once did we try to peg the speedometer, but as the needle slid beyond 120 and the engine was still pulling strong, we backed off.

In compliance with the rule at the proving ground facility (a member of the engineering staff must accompany all visiting drivers), a genial ruddy-complexioned fellow

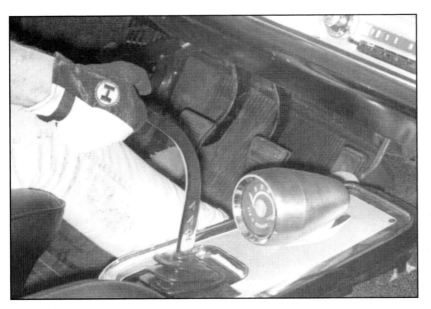

And then there's the Hurst shifter, smooth with or without glove. Tach and console are extras.

named Jerry Liles took part on the runs and directed our attention to various interest points during our track time. He also commented in passing about the fact that the 442s mill was identical to the 425 except for the smaller bore. Later on we learned that the 425-type pistons are identical in weight to their smaller counterparts, so no rebalancing would be necessary for the switch.

Given these facts it is the next logical step to wonder why Olds didn't just use the 425-inch engine to begin with, or at least list it as an option; the reason being, of course, that the GM "front office" drew the cubic inch line at 400 in the A-bodied car, of which the 442 is a member, hence the smaller engine. Another consideration may have been that the 442 had just about the right balance carrying a 400 cube mill, so why stretch the car's capabilities. We'd have to concur with this judgment in all but race course conditions because there is seldom any instance in the course of normal driving where the 442 potential can be used as it is, let alone with 25 additional inches.

With our test track trials concluded, we adjourned to the water-trough area to see how well the car was sealed against moisture. First run through the drink at 15 miles per hour produced no signs of leakage and a nonsensational shot for our photo editor. So we went back to have at it again, this time "at speed." Running through the trough in such a confined area creates strange effects as Eric Rickman discovered when a wall of water advanced through his viewfinder. A few drops crept into the Olds passenger compartment around the dimmer switch hole on this run but it was nothing that a little dum-dum wouldn't correct in a jiffy—a remedy, we might add, more rapidly accomplished than the time it took Rick to dry off.

With our mission accomplished, we settled back for the demonstrations that were well worth an hour out of anyone's schedule and then prepared for the trip to L. A. via Yuma. During all this desert travel the 442 never faltered, and at night, when the temperature sags far enough to ice-coat small bodies of water, the Olds heating system functioned with an efficiency able to scorch the tail off a jack-rabbit at 40 paces. Although we never ran into any weather above 80, the ventilating quality of the car seemed to be adequate for all but those 120-degree days when nothing satisfies like an air conditioner.

On the trip back to home base the miles-per-gallon picture shone brighter with every tankful and finally climbed to more than 16, despite the fact that the driving pace had not slackened. By this juncture we had also learned that the seat angle, which had on first sight appeared to be overly rearward inclined, was in reality just what the doctor ordered for long spells in the saddle, especially in conjunction with the adjustable steering wheel. The accelerator pedal had a comfortable angle too and, since it was on the same plane with the brake, quick stops were easily accomplished by pivoting the right foot on the heel from one to the other. Travel on the individually adjusted bucket seats was more than adequate even for six-footers but, when all the way back, they were knee knockers for those in the back.

Besides the steering, the single most attractive fixture in the cockpit was the floor-shift handle placement and operation. The stick was one of the best placed of any in an American car and would shift fast or slow with equal ease. A little more plush for the average buyer would probably be the optional console alluded to previously, but our preference ran to the small black rubber boot molded into the floor mat on our car. It somehow seemed more in keeping with the machine's no-nonsense character.

Back in L. A. and surrounding locales, we drove the 442 in virtually all city situations and never found it unpredictable. On rain-slick streets the car always exhibited good road-sticking characteristics—except on acceleration from dead starts when a slightly overzealous foot was applied to the accelerator and the rear wheels tended to slip a bit in some cases. Outside of the few drops that were forced through during our splash test, not even the heaviest downpour caused any wetness inside. The electric wipers function very efficiently, sweeping clear a wide windshield arc with each stroke. And the front glass itself was tinted down from the roof about four inches to reduce glare considerably.

The local driving phase of our test also included an opportunity to check out the 442 on some 0-60 sprints, which averaged out to just about six seconds for a series of tries on different surfaces. As another portion of each car's evaluation, we like to run at a regular drag strip and in competition if possible. On the particular Sunday that we went out to San Fernando Raceway the first big meet of the 1965 season came off and this, coupled with a trip to the hospital to patch up a deep cut that was inflicted by a razor-sharp fender edge, effectively cut the number of runs to one. For the single blast, we got off at the first wink of the green light, but the tires just didn't want to get a decent grip so the elapsed time went up in smoke at a disappointing 16.38 seconds. Another 442 identical to ours, except for cheater slicks, ran out at 14.15 seconds, clearing the lights at 98 miles per hour, and we'd guess this is nearer the actual "stock" potential.

Most interesting of all the Olds entries on hand that day (and there were many) was a '64 Cutlass with the smaller 330-inch engine, a dyno-tuned job, 12.5:1 buckets, and a big Holley four-throat, which wrung out a quick 12.68-second elapsed time at a creditable 109 miles per hour. Sponsored by Guy Martin Oldsmobile, the car had been beaten only a few times in class and amassed 30 trophies in meets all over southern California. With 70 more cubes and the improvements of the newer design engine, the '65 442 should really haul when set up properly.

Our own times disclosed that the car ran faster with two on board than one and this emphasized the observation that the machine has too much low-end torque to run at its maximum capabilities on the strip without better bite. The average driver probably will not find this situation painfully hard to accept, however, because dragging is only a small portion of the 442's attraction. Fantastic handling with just the right amount of oversteer, high-speed touring potential, and generally sound construction minus frill are the features that will sell the car.

Emphatically, the 442 remained one of the most likeable machines we have ever had the pleasure to drive. At the going base price of $2,799.02 f.o.b. Detroit, this Olds is really a buyer's bargain; we wish there were more of them.

GTO

ERIC DAHLQUIST
Hot Rod, July 1965

are the three letters Pontiac has made synonymous with performance and youth. In stock or hot trim, for the road or on the drag strip, the three-carb Tiger is a versatile charger, light on its feet, has phenomenal top end potential and, in short, lives up to its reputation

"Giddy-up, giddy-up, giddy-up, GTO." So goes the opening stanza of the million-seller recorded by Jan and Dean that some have said has gone a long way toward immortalizing Pontiac's jazzed-up Tiger as the machine of machines for American youth. Whether or not this ditty has measurably increased the car's popularity or not, everyone and his brother has tested, wrung out, raced, and rebuilt it to a point where there's hardly anything left unsaid. In light of this situation, we elected to conduct an evaluation, but with a slightly different wrinkle than previous tests. Take one GTO Tiger (as the car has been nicknamed from another ballad, sung, appropriately enough, by the Tigers) in showroom shape and then another, whose tail has been bobbed slightly for a quicker pulse, and compare them: stock vs. hot.

This whole project could and did become a bit complicated before we were through, but it turned out to be quite enlightening, too. When all the arrangements were settled, we wound up with a silver-blue metallic hardtop and an all-white two-door sedan. Outwardly the difference in both cars' appearance was only a set of alloy wheels that were mounted on the white job, but under the sheet metal there was a difference of night and day.

The first thing you do when you get your hands on one of these bombs is to lift the hood for an inspection as well as an exhibition. There it is, 389 cubic inches of go, topped with three 2CG Rochesters that are capped with shimmering chrome-plated, nonrestrictive air filters. In outward appearance at least, it is readily apparent that the powerplant is of the same illustrious family that Fireball Roberts blazed to victory on Daytona's high banks, or that Jim Wangers won top stock with at the nationals in 1960. In the GTO you can get either a four-barrel 335 horsepower version or the three deuces job that sports 25 additional ponies and a nutty, custom-looking, nonfunctional hood scoop that really shatters the drive-in set.

Both our cars had the optional engines, which really represent only a small portion on an available extra parts list as long as your arm. Things like 10.75-to-1 compression, a

The clean design of the GTO is evident against the backdrop of the desert. For extended use on remote, washboard side roads, a handling package is needed.

cam that sports .406-inch lift intakes and .408-inch lift exhausts, and bigger 1.657-inch diameter valves are some of the subtle touches that breathe extra life into the Tiger as compared to the milder Tempests and Le Mans. The more docile of the two test machines came equipped with air conditioning and therefore was outfitted with the 3.23 differential ratio as prescribed by the manufacturer. Because there is the chance that we'd become entangled in a morass of intricate comparisons, we'll talk generally about the showroom car first and then turn the microscope on the hotted-up version.

The blue hardtop's interior was stitched up in all-black motif with an imitation wood applique on the dash around the instrumentation. We were never quite able to determine if the eight-grand tach in the car is standard, but very few GTOs are without one and it represents a worthwhile addition in any case. Also looking like wood was the rim on the rather small steering wheel that, with the aid of power, needed only 4.2 spins lock to lock and felt just right in conjunction with well-placed bucket seats. Not quite so handy was the Hurst shifter that treaded through an attractive console to the standard four-speed box with ratios of 2.56:1 for first; 1.91:1 for second; 1.48:1 for third; and 1.00:1 for fourth.

The competition version of GTO has relatively plain interior, and the close-ratio transmission option places the shifter in more favorable position to the driver than a normal Tiger.

The transmission shifted well enough, but the handle was just too far forward to manipulate without stretching. Electrically-operated window lifts were one accessory that we grew to admire, not because of any inherent laziness on our part but for the fact that with the seatbelt fastened, it is well-nigh impossible for the driver to reach across to the opposite door to raise or lower the windows by hand.

Some amazing things occur when you get this 115-inch wheelbase animal on the road, not the least of which is the admiring glances passed out, especially from the young people. It's plain enough from the strategically-placed insignia that the car is a GTO, but that cool hood scoop marks it as the three-carb charger. On twisty, short-radius-turn

Plusher with air conditioning and power windows, a stocker is easy to drive and has excellent top speed, thanks to 3.23 rear-end ratio.

roads, where driving as the average person would, the car handled beautifully; it tracked well and went where it was pointed without complaint. Increase the speed from 40 to about 55 or 60 miles per hour in an identical situation and that big hunk of cast iron under the bonnet begins to exert Newtonian influences, causing noticeable understeer. We should interject here that Pontiac has a heavy-duty handling package and, as installed on the other white Tiger, raised cornering potential measurably.

All the GTOs with air, as noted earlier, have the 3.23 rear end and this, coupled with the progressive carburetor arrangement, allows some advantages and one drawback over other configurations. The car cruises phenomenally well, easily in excess of 90 miles per

The car's detailing is also very good.

hour if asked, on just the center two-throat alone and does it economically. At a sustained 75, we recorded slightly over 15.5 miles per gallon on relatively uninterrupted stretches of touring. Because of the lively response on the single job, a woman driver or someone with a light foot would never know an extra pair of carbs was lying out there just down the line a bit farther on the accelerator. Conversely, however, a self-styled hot dog who likes to have everything hanging out, continually opening all the butterflies at low speed, will ultimately do himself in because the engine just can't use all the gas at low rpm and some residue will

It's plain enough from the strategically-placed insignia that the car is a GTO, but that cool hood scoop marks it as the three-carb charger.

wind up in the oil pan, effectively thinning the lubricant. The idea is to treat the setup as it was designed to be used and no problems will be encountered.

Normal springing notwithstanding, the car feels exceptionally secure at high speeds. Even with the needle swinging past 125 out on one of southern California's dry lakes (and the engine still pulling), there is no dangerous floating and the stiff springs are even better. On washboard dirt surfaces, however, the machine is skittish as a young colt and even the handling package doesn't represent the ultimate solution. This condition won't represent a serious handicap for most GTO buyers, however, because there aren't many populous areas that have scores of these jarring lanes left anymore. In short, our stocker did just about all the things it was supposed to, and in excellent form at that.

The white GTO was set up for competition, taking full advantage of the abundant part options. The engine was basically identical to our strictly stocker but with one critical difference: it had been Bobcatized.

In less generic parlance, this meant that Royal Oak Pontiac's (Royal Oak, Michigan) high-performance kit consisting of a quicker centrifugal distributor advance, thin head gaskets, blocked heat riser gasket, larger .070 carburetor jets, fiber insert rocker-arm-stud lock

GTO stands for *Gran Turismo Omologato*. You've probably heard of it. A Pontiac in a saber-toothed tiger skin. The deceptively beautiful body comes in convertible, sports coupe, and hardtop configurations. With pinstriping. On a heavy-duty suspension system that thinks it's married to the ground. Bucket seats and carpeting. Wood-grained dash. Redlines or whitewalls at no extra cost. Chromed 335-hp 4-barrel under the hood. Fully-synchronized 3-speed on the column. Or order a heavy-duty all-synchro 3-speed or 4-speed with Hurst floor shifter. Or 2-speed auto. Or the 360-hp 3 2-BBL. There's a catalog full of options. See if you can get your Pontiac dealer to cough one up. That's the GTO/2+2 performance catalog. You'll recognize it. It vibrates.

Speak softly and carry a GTO

Pontiac Motor Division • General Motors Corporation

An ad promoting the GTO.

nuts, and high-output oil pump had been installed. By way of supplement, a neat set of headers by Doug ensured that exhaust gases would exit in the most expeditious, as well as noisiest, fashion.

Broken down separately, the individual pieces each had a specific purpose. The distributor alteration allowed the curve to come in fast at around 1,000 rpm and be all finished at 3,000. Total advance was held at 34 degrees and did not to exceed 36 in any case. The thin head gaskets (.027–.035-inch, compared to .054-inch normally) hike compression to 11.23-to-1. Blocking the heat riser speaks for itself as do the larger jets. The fiber insert lock nuts allow rpm to exceed the stock 5,500 limit by about 500, while the oil pump helps keep the engine in one piece for sustained competition periods.

All these things had been done to the powerplant previously and approximately 5,000 miles of normal driving were logged, including several drag dates, before we received the car. We had neither the time nor the opportunity for a complete check to see if everything was functioning properly, but we did add a fresh set of spark plugs and checked the distributor curve. In addition, while the .070 jets fitted all the way through the Rochesters may be suitable for the damper and cooler East, it is too much for the primary carb in the drier West, so the stock .063-inch primaries were put back in to lean the mixture out to comply with the conditions at hand.

You can defer for an aluminum-cased, close-ratio four-speed in the GTO and our drag model had it with cogs of 2.20:1 in first gear, 1.64:1 in second gear, 1.28:1 in third gear, and 1.1:1 for fourth. And where the other shifter was a little too far forward, the one on this box was perfect. The rear-axle ratio was a beaut at 4.33 or just what you need for instant out-of-the-gate shots with a set of 8.50x14-inch M&H slicks on the back. As a final touch, two Air-Lifts installed in the rear coils gave the opportunity for some tries at chassis jacking for better bite.

Despite these modifications, the rule makers have put their stamp of approval on the operation so the car competed as described in B or C/Stock, depending what association you run. On the road, the pepped-up Tiger eats more gas due mostly, one suspects, to the relatively high rpm necessitated by the 4.33, but even hard driving doesn't lower the figure much below 10 miles per gallon. And increased engine noise isn't really a problem either because, for one reason, solid lifters aren't part of the deal and, for another, sound deadening is pretty good in the body.

One thing is sure, however: in modern freeway traffic the short gear gives such good response that's just the ticket for changing lanes with room to spare or getting out of tight spots. When you hit all three carburetors, the sock is unreal.

Since one of the objects of our evaluation was definitely a thorough strip session, we packed tools, extra parts, and cameras aboard the Tigers and made a beeline for San Fernando Raceway on the first free weekend. No attempt was made to super-tune the stock Wide-Track, other than making sure everything was functioning properly. The performer, by contrast, was ready for on-the-spot adjustments of any sort should they be necessary. The Bobcat kit is supplied with Champion J-10 spark plugs, and we had a new set of these, plus another of Autolite's comparable A-42 range, both gapped at .030-inch. After getting all unnecessary weight unloaded, we decided to run both cars off together to see what the real difference in setup was. This necessitated the enlistment of an additional driver and, because someone extra sharp at dragging was more than just slightly desirable, we were fortunate in obtaining the services of none other than veteran AA/Fuel pilot Mike Snively, who, incidentally, later in the day turned out to be Top Eliminator at the helm of Ed Pink's "Old Master" rail.

Mike did a commendable job, but when the L. L. went green, there just wasn't any way that the stocker could equal the "tuned" version. With 4.33s pulling strong, our "racer" went on to win, with headers corked, at 95 miles per hour in 15.40 seconds. Mike hit a creditable 90 miles per hour in 16.50, which wasn't bad considering the 3.23 long-screw in the rear. Later on, after uncapping the headers and getting accustomed to the car a bit more, we got the hot Tiger down to around the 14-seconds-flat area at between 102–103 miles per hour. The engine ran flawlessly on every run, but despite the fact that we were never dumped out of the gate, the elapsed time wasn't quite enough to match the class leaders. The main difference between our car and the GTO that finally got the gold was the little matter of a thorough blueprint job and engine balancing, which seems to be the key in cracking out 12-second elapsed times.

Our trip to the strip brought out several points of consideration. For one thing, the GTO stock posted one of the quickest as-is quarter-mile performances we have found in this year's *Hot Rod* road testing program. We must quickly mention, however, that this isn't quite good enough for serious weekend racing. True, in some areas of the country the Bobcat treatment will be sufficient to beat the pack, but to do the job right it is apparent that an engine rebuild along the lines of blueprinting and balance is a must. This isn't a blotch on the GTO potential because every car we've tested has had the same problem.

In all, the GTO is a fun-to-drive machine, hot or stock. Success formulas are elusive creatures at best, but Pontiac seems to have at least part of the market cornered for the time being. For some, this era appears indeed to be the years of the Quick-Wide-Track.

MUSTANG WITH FANGS. . .GT-350

ERIC RICKMAN
Hot Rod, August 1965

Carroll Shelby puts his Cobra's sting in America's most popular sports car—with jarring results

There's a story that's been around awhile to the effect that if you cross a parrot with a tiger there is apt to be some doubt about just exactly what you'll get . . . but when it talks, you'd better listen! This is somewhat the position that Carroll Shelby finds himself in after crossing a Cobra with a Mustang; the Cobra venom has given Ford's sporty little workhorse considerably more authority, enough to call it a race car.

To have a car "homologated" (accepted and classified) by FIA, the international governing body of automobile racing, certain rules must be observed. To establish a car as a production model, a hundred or more must be built and sold. Once the car has been homologated, changes are permitted in the engine and drive train, or the chassis, but not in both. This meant that Shelby had the choice of building 100 all-out race cars, and trying to sell them, or building a few race cars and making the remainder street machines to be sold to the lucky public. With chassis or engine changes being the only alterations permitted, he chose to produce all the cars with a racing chassis and concentrate only on engine changes between the street and racing versions.

The street machine provided to *Hot Rod* is rated at 306 horsepower, packing a 289-ci Cobra engine. The competition version pulls 350 horses from the same engine with the installation of an optional cam, increased compression, port modification, etc., plus some mighty fine tuning that adds 44 horsepower. The bare makins for both the street and competition versions are sent to Shelby's Los Angeles production line less hood, engine, and rear seat. Stock high-performance engines arrive in crates and go directly to the engine department where they are converted to Cobras. High-riser manifold and center-pivot Holley carburetor are fitted; the latter eliminates stall on turns and is rated at 718 cubic-feet-per-minute airflow. Ford dual-point high-performance ignition with centrifugal advance is next, along with the Cobra six-quart, finned, cast aluminum oil pan, and rocker arm covers of similar material and motif. A set of 1 1/2-inch i.d. headers that

Even in a full broadside, the Mustang GT has all four wheels planted squarely on the ground. The one-inch front stabilizer bar holds body roll to a minimum and the oversize Goodyear 7.75x15 Blue Dot tires show no roll-under.

mate to a 2-inch exhaust system completes the engine package. This Cobra treatment raises the stock engine's horsepower from 271 to 306.

Chassis and body modifications are more involved. Beginning at the front, the upper A-arms are lowered an inch to drop the roll center and effect slight negative camber for high-speed turns. A stabilizer bar of 1-inch diameter is installed to reduce body lean under the same conditions. Longer pitman and idler arms reduce steering wheel travel from 4 to 3 1/2 turns lock to lock (19:1 ratio). Ford's Kelsey-Hayes spot brakes with DS-11 lining are used on the front wheels.

The rear end really gets a working-over. Shelby's Mustangs arrive with the Galaxy high-performance rear end and brakes already in place, but they are switched to 2 1/2-inch wide metallic brake shoes and a NoSPIN center section. This special center section has no differential action, working on an actuating ramp and dog clutch principle. When the load from an axle overrides the power input from the pinion gear, such as encountered during slow cornering when the outside rear wheel must travel farther, a ramp mechanism slips and disengages the dog clutch teeth on the overriding axle, allowing it

The finned aluminum Cobra pan serves as oil cooler as well as providing extra capacity. The engine location remains unchanged.

to turn free. When cornering under power, however, and the pinion gear is feeding more power than the outboard axle, the ramp setup can't slip and the clutch remains engaged, effecting a locked rear end, which is ideal for racing but not street use.

To absorb torque and prevent spring wrap-up, traction bars are installed above the rear-axle housing. To limit body lift, a steel cable attached to the body is looped under each axle housing. Slowing this movement also are heavier Koni shock absorbers on all four wheels. As an option, Shelby-Cragar 15-inch aluminum wheels are available. In either dress, all GTs are equipped with Goodyear Blue Dot High Performance 7.75x15 tires.

Body changes, along with a grille facelift, include a cowl brace and reinforcement of the shock tower area. The battery is moved to the trunk, and a fiberglass hood incorporating an air scoop is fitted over the engine compartment. Interior alterations consist primarily of the removal of the rear seat and the installation of a fiberglass deck carrying the spare tire (the rear seat is removed to conform with the Sports Car Club of

The stock brake appears at left. The two-and-a half-inch-wide replacement uses metallic linings. A heavy foot is needed because there is no power assist. Braking of the light car is fantastic.

Forward mounting of the traction bar is on the top of the frame as in a Corvette. The pivot point of the mount is directly over the forward spring eye, thereby giving correct parallelogram geometry and avoiding any binding action as the axle moves.

Front binders are made by Kelsey-Hayes for Ford. This is the optional unit available on stock Mustangs. The GT features DS-11 brake pucks, which are harder and contain some sintered metal. These will withstand severe use.

The NoSPIN rear end has no differential action. It is basically a dog clutch assembly. Over-riding axle torque causes the ramp system to disengage the axle. If drive torque is greater, the unit locks up.

America's definition of a sports car). To keep the driver informed, a supplemental instrument cluster with tach and oil gage is bolted to the upper edge of the dash.

The finished product weighs 2,800 pounds at the curb, with 53/47 percent distribution respectively, front and rear. Price out the door for the street car is $4,547 plus tax and license, while the fire-breathin' competition job is definitely in the ballpark as far as racing jobs go at $5,950 plus tax. And if you do go for the race model, here's their exciting list of extras, in addition to the aforementioned group: blueprinted engine with racing cam, engine oil cooler, cold air plenum chamber between carbs and hood scoop, extra-capacity radiator, even larger straight-through exhausts, front and rear brake cooling ducts, 34-gallon fuel tank with 3 1/2-inch quick-fill cap, electric fuel pump, magnesium wheels with 7-inch rims, roll bar with shoulder harness, fully instrumented dash, wrap-around bucket seats, fiberglass bumpers and apron, Plexiglas windows, fireproof interior

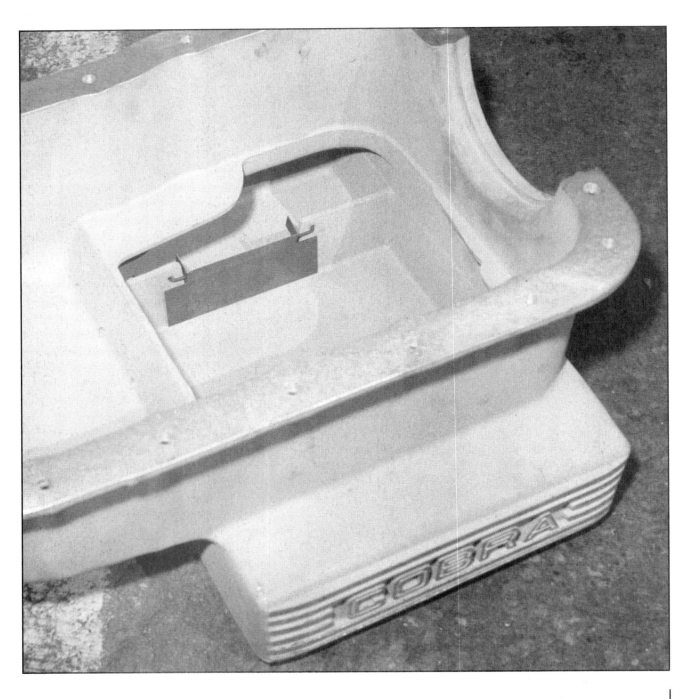

Cobra's six-quart oil pan has interior baffling at the sides as well as at midpoint. The check valve–type flappers ensure oil supply to the pump, even in severe cornering.

with extinguisher, and several other refinements. Even with this added, the competition version has a curb weight of only 2,550 pounds.

With lots of rubber on the ground, and a near 50/50 weight distribution, the GT-350 corners as though it were on the proverbial rails; rather than spin it prefers to move into a four-wheel drift. The feeling is one of being in full command at all times. Shelby's street

The rear traction bar mounting is a yoke welded to the axle housing. Again the pivot point is directly in line with center of the axle. Heavy-duty Koni shocks and a steel cable tie-down limit the body's vertical travel.

version is docile enough for everyday driving, with the possible exception that it steers a bit heavy and rides rather stiffly. It's long on performance, idles down smoothly, and still punches out from zero to 60 in 5.7 seconds. The brakes, in combination with the big tires, bring the GT down in one big hurry. It does take a heavy foot, however, since there is no power assist to detract from the true feel of what's going on at the wheels.

One final incentive to some is the fact that NHRA has placed the GT-350 in B/Sports category, so you're all ready to drag. We guarantee you won't fall asleep while driving this one, and it'll give anything you're liable to encounter fits, particularly those in the "other" camp.

HOW HOT THE HEMI?

ERIC DAHLQUIST
Hot Rod, December 1965

*Dodge drops a 426-ci street hemi in its Coronet and upgrades
the transmission, rear end, brakes, and suspension to concoct one
of the fastest and most fantastic sedans ever*

Since the days of the first one-cylinder runabouts, and even before that, the honor of owning the hottest rig in town has carried with it considerable prestige among the young, or young at heart. How often this superiority was brought to force usually depended upon the number of qualified challengers or, perhaps, merely the fierce sound or appearance of the reputed king, not to mention the efficiency of the local constable's mount.

Little has changed with the passing of time; from Ted's Woodward Avenue Drive-In in Detroit to Bob's Van Nuys Boulevard "Big Boy" emporium in Los Angeles, the question of the hottest machine in town is still the vital topic . . . and it can make or break a new Detroit model. Up to September of this year, the ranking order was pretty much established as to who was top dog, or maybe top tiger would be more appropriate, but then a hemi was loosed by Dodge and the order of command was knocked into a cocked hat.

Dodge had a pretty good image going back in 1963 when the "street wedge" first was offered but, for a variety of reasons, paramount of which was the fact that the car lost a lot of its sting on the subsequent model run, the brand fell rapidly from the throne. Recalling this, there was fear in some quarters that when the hemi was detuned for street use, it might slip into mediocrity. Another notion cautioned that the car might be fine for driving as long as it were only in a straight line with no sudden stops or turns to contend with. These could have been serious reservations but, as we shall see in the Coronet, no such speculations were qualified.

But let's go back to the middle of September when Dodge Public Relations Chief Frank Wylie invited us to investigate the new definition in high-performance motoring the company was offering. This was just before the new '66 model lines were introduced, so driving one on the street was understandably out of the question. The gates of the spacious Chrysler proving ground in Chelsea, Michigan, had been thrown open to us for pictures and some road work, but we still yearned for the opportunity to know how the

Coming 'round the bend at speed, the super-bomb displayed a marked tendency to stay in the groove. In hard cornering, the car had mild understeer, which became oversteer as more power was applied.

car lived in everyday situations, idled at traffic lights, moved through in-town congestion, and sang down the open road. Despite the release date and a scarcity of street hemis in general, a light shone in the darkness. A number of '65s had been equipped with the potent powerplant to thoroughly check out the combination before it was deemed acceptable for public consumption, and we were fortunate to get one to use during our stay in Detroit. It was mechanically identical to a '66 except that the engine manifold was water heated instead of exhaust warmed as the production ones would be.

When we got to Detroit Metropolitan Airport, it was a warm Saturday evening, just the kind of night for an adventure in motoring. So we went directly to our goal, the Dodge garage on Campau Avenue, where our street hemi was patiently waiting to be unleashed. It was in there all right, innocent looking even though the four-ply 7.75x14 low-cord angle blackwalls were hubcapless. These nylons, bigger than any found on the Dodge passenger line but available at extra cost, were the first tipoff that the Coronet was special from the ground up, not merely a hashed-together stocker with a big powerplant dumped in and nothing else. We stowed the luggage, slipped the ignition key home, and with several revolutions of the starter brought the engine to life. Or maybe the key wasn't even needed the way the powerplant sounded—fierce and taut noises echoed in the dim garage light. The 4.25x3.75-inch bore and stroke engine, rated at 490 pounds of torque and 425 horsepower, started easily and idled acceptably well. Pull the Torqueflite lever

A 60-mile-per-hour jump on a toboggan-run road failed to dim our enthusiasm of the car.

into drive and there is a solid thud as the car immediately strains against the pressure of the parking brake. The already top-notch three-speeder has been beefed for its new task, beefed to handle the greater torque characteristics of the hemi. The steering ratio is a quick 16:1, and it doesn't require arms the size of a stevedore to get the car unparked even in a cramped garage area because it's power assisted. Once free of the garage and onto the highway, there was a temptation to punch it, make the progressive linkage snap back to its last stop, open the rear two barrels of the back Carter 3140 AFB, and then all four barrels of the last carb, and then all eight barrels of both AFBs. It all happens in a 60th of a minute and the Torqueflite shifts down into low. Everything explodes! There is a frantic sound of huge quantities of the soft night air being rammed through eight venturis and the sound of rubber and a shift from first to second so positive it scares you. The Coronet has to be this way or it won't make it with the in-group who influences the out group who buys the cars.

We headed out toward Woodward Avenue to just drive the car for a while, probably in a manner which will represent most of its life. The Coronet hemi has big 11x3-inch brakes up front and 11x2 1/2-inch at the rear instead of 11x2 1/2 straight through like the stocker. For a time there was a movement afoot to make sintered metallic brakes an option, but in the interests of consistency, 11 3/16-inch Bendix caliper disc brakes were chosen; both the A- and C-bodied Dodge lines have them. They are to be used on the front only with 10x2 1/2-inch rear drums plus a proportioning valve to equalize braking efficiency between the unlike systems, disc, and drum.

Even with the stock street hemi braking package, the stopping ability is well within the acceptable range, and the brakes do not fade out when warm or get grabby after a few stops. It's nice to see that the engineers in product planning have done their homework in delivering adequate anchors for their speedy sedan instead of forcing the buyer to take the options to be safe.

With the heavier hemi up front instead of the popular 318-ci V-8, the Coronet doesn't feel nose-heavy at all. However, it well might have if certain subtle improvements hadn't been made in the suspension. The front torsion bar thickness was upped from .88-inch diameter to .92, which in turn caused the wheel rate to rise from 120 pounds per inch to 140. Where the stock Coronet has no sway bar and the optional one is .84-inch diameter, the hemi version is .94. One more rear spring leaf has been added, bringing the total to 5.5 and a wheel rate of 170 pounds per inch over a usual 120. Another effect of this stiffening is that the front roll rate (expressed in pounds per inch) has been doubled at 240 while the rear was bumped to 145.

In terms of actual riding quality, all these figures add up to a journey that is not jarring or harsh but firm and secure, even while diving on the brakes on a reverse camber turn. The rear springs look comfortably hefty and, because of their strength and design, no traction bars are necessary to prevent wheel hop on either full power starts or stops. This goes against the grain of some enthusiasts, who cannot feel happy unless they see a set of trusswork arms underneath their car of equivalent strength to support a good two-lane highway creek crossing. But the fact is that the tops of all stock car racers, the Ramchargers, have never used them on any of their Dodges.

Underneath, the anti-roll bar diameter has been bumped to .94-inch, .010-inch greater than normal. The brakes used in front are 11x3, while 11x2 1/2-inch brakes are on the rear.

You can't drive a wolf in sheep's clothing like this without getting reactions, and the most frequent was the question of what was in it. We pulled into a gas station and the inevitable oil check drew a small knot of interested young spectators. There before them in the bluish illumination was a compartment filled with authority, its block painted bright orange with black crackle-finish valve covers and a giant chrome, nonrestrictive air cleaner that snuggles around both carburetors. There was the new boss. Suddenly whatever they were driving was one down on the ladder of their acceptance.

They wanted to know if it was really as fast as it looked, about keeping the solids adjusted, and about the rear-end ratio and strength. In most of the hot compacts, the delicate rear-axle story is pretty grim because they tend to wear out quickly, but not the Coronet. It has a 9 3/4-inch ring gear, the biggest in the industry, to go behind the super heavy-duty A-833 four-speed. The ring gear in the automatic is an inch smaller. Ratios are 3.54 and 3.23, respectively.

Over the top of a 32 percent grade comes 426 inches of bounding Coronet, easily leaving behind the lower reaches of the Chelsea, Michigan, proving ground.

The next day we hit the trail early for the Chelsea proving grounds, which is about a good hour's drive west of the city on Interstate 94. This probably is as average a stretch of turnpike driving as you'll find—gently rolling in some places, straight and flat in others—but it was gobbled up by the Coronet. Passing was a cinch, and this is an understatement. Response is always immediate, getting you from behind slower-moving vehicles with ridiculous blasting ease that leaves the uninitiated with a sagging jaw. We arrived at the Chelsea gate knowing that the street hemi has excellent road manners and no tendency to porpoise along at speed.

Now we switched to the '66 Coronet, a deep maroon convertible which, as mentioned before, was identical to the '65 in all mechanical respects except for the manifold heating method. Jumping from one to another really allowed a graphic comparison in advances Dodge had made in styling and safety. Body sheet metal is quite unlike the previous models, and we noticed immediately that seating position had improved markedly. In the '65, the wheel position had always felt a bit too high, but in the '66 it was fine. Either the seat had been raised or the wheel lowered, or a combination of both, which accomplished the job. They also did away with the vertical door handles in favor of those that operate horizontally, pulling out from the door to minimize accidental opening.

Quality control is one area that Dodge has always prided itself on, and it was obvious that even this first new model had plenty of attention during assembly. All the interior moldings were attached properly and no examples of loose thread or flapping vinyl material could be found, even at the bottom edge of the paneling. Nineteen sixty-four was the last year that Dodge had its push-button arrangement for the automatic, so our "rag top" came with the selector on the column. The other machine had the optional floor shifter and it would be our preference of the two because it's more positive. Dash layout is all very well taken and the only "blinkin'" light on the panel is the high-beam indicator.

The top goes up or down with no fuss, and this is one of the few cars in which provision has been made to allow the assembly to fold far enough into the well to allow a noncamel's hump profile with the cover boot on.

A good deal of the endurance testing that goes into each new Dodge product is accomplished at Chelsea because they have every conceivable type of road condition on which to flog the cars—hilly, flat, straight, twisting, concrete, asphalt, gravel gauntlets that will show a car's true mettle. So we set off through this labyrinth to get some idea of how the '66 Coronet behaved and record the whole bit on film.

One particularly revealing section was an undulating road that swept over some small hills. We made several runs over this section, beginning at around 50 and finally building courage and speed enough at 65 to get all four wheels high off the ground. The interesting scene was that after you landed on the downside of the highest hill, there still remained the task of bringing the car to a safe halt on a roller-coaster slope. Also, when you launch over one-and-a-half tons of anything, it is likely to come down with a bang. Fortunately, the good suspension stability of the Coronet and a front skid plate thoughtfully placed under the engine got us through in one piece and none the worse for wear.

One thing we did notice, however, was that the gas got sloshed around so much in the carburetor float bowls that the engine died on two occasions. This situation doesn't seem to pose much of a handicap, though, because the likelihood of running over such terrain at the speed we did won't be too frequent. The only other place we noticed something similar was when ripping into a fairly tight corner and then clamping on the binders. As the car was hauled down abruptly, it tended to sputter momentarily. Our other car didn't behave this way at all so we suspect that float levels may have been a trifle too low. And while on the topic of turns, we have to mention that this Coronet will get through them in a hurry with a manageable amount of understeer that progresses to oversteer as the accelerator is pushed further to the wood.

Finally, we wanted to run the car through the quarter-mile to see just how accurately the belt in the back correlated with the time on the clock. The proving ground has a couple of quarter-miles marked off, one with a set of timers, but there was no one around to operate them so we made our tries with two people on board against a hand-held stopwatch.

A lot of people will get to know the clean Coronet rear-end design as more hemis roll off the line.

In case you haven't found out yet, the only way to get these high-performance stocks off the line in anything resembling a decent fashion, without a complete chassis tune job and super soft tires, is to bog-start 'em. That is, keep the rpm down until you're under way and then stand on it. Even so, the standard skins are just not the hot setup for ultimate traction, so we didn't get the best of all possible times. At that, the convertible with low miles registered on the odometer popped a number of 14.60 elapsed times, feeling as if it didn't quite have the finest edge on tune. The '65 had been run many more miles, was understandably freer, and had the advantage of less weight by about 100 pounds (3,345–3,240 pound shipping weights, respectively). Now the elapsed time dipped to the low 14s, even with "bald eagles" on the rear. We cannot vouch for the accuracy of the speedometer, but it registered between 105–110, which can't be too bad.

Performance like this is not to be found in too many other areas. Drop the weight of the passenger, add a set of slicks that the car desperately needs for competition, and you've got a good 13-second machine stock. Now, since this sounds pretty good, we'll keep going. Later on in the year, Dodge will offer a high-performance package for the street hemi consisting of headers and a few other goodies. Zowie, 12 seconds! And under present conditions this Coronet should run in AA/Stock unless, of course, the rules get revised. Here it looks like a sure winner.

And if a fellow were to get a set of the aluminum heads, or magnesium heads and manifold—or even, perish the thought, the injectors—it wouldn't take much more to go match racing. Actually this isn't as farfetched as it seems because, although the street hemi engine is detuned, it shares much in common with the all-out racing cars.

However, it is heavier. The manifold and heads are cast iron, as is the oil pump and the water pump housing. These are aluminum or magnesium on competition versions. Also, cam timing is cooled down from 312 degrees duration to 276 and the compression ratio from 12.5:1 to 10.25:1. Carburetion is by two Carter four-throats with primaries at 1.44 inches and secondaries 1.69 inches. The competition version uses a pair of 1 11/16 Holley R-3116s on a short ram manifold or an injector setup.

But after that, the differences are about exhausted. The street version has the horizontal, tie-bolted main bearing caps (cross bolted) and the crankshaft is hard 1046 carbon steel with shot-peened fillets and dipped nitriding treatment to help provide fatigue resistance. Connecting rods are forged steel with pressed fit piston pins. Stellite-faced valves retain the large head (2.25-inch intakes and 1.94-inch exhausts) to stem diameter (.309-inch and .308-inch, respectively) ratio that helps reduce valve train inertia. Cantilever constructed rocker arms are light and long and provide the simple jam nut-type adjusting provision for lash that allows the "set-it-and-forget-it" idea. Inner and outer valve springs are provided to allow revs to 6,300 rpm. It has a lot going for it.

And that's about the inside scoop on the street hemi that will almost certainly be the standard of comparison for some time to come. Two things will sell this car more than anything else—the sight of Coronet taillights disappearing into the distance ahead and slipping behind the wheel of the winged vehicle itself. The first time you get on it hard you're hooked: that sudden rush of speed, of roaring venturii, of fantastic shifts, of being the fastest.

1966 CORONET

	V-8 First Option (Most Popular Coronet Engine)	Highest Performance Regular Production Option
ENGINE		
Engine Displacement (ci)	318	426 Hemi
Power, Horsepower @ RPM:	230 @ 4,400	425 @ 5,000
Torque, FT. LB. @ RPM:	340 @ 2,400	490 @ 5,000
Compression Ratio	9.0	10.25
Carburetor	2-barrel	2—4-barrel
Throttle Bore Dia. (in.)	1.44	Primary 1.44 Secondary 1.69
Camshaft Duration:		
Intake	244	276
Exhaust	240	276
Intake Valve Diameter (in.)	1.84	2.25
Exhaust Valve Diameter (in.)	1.56	1.94
Exhaust:	Single	Dual
Exhaust Diameters (in.)		
Exhaust Pipe	1.75 (Branch) 2.00 (Main)	2.25
Muffler	Reverse Flow	Reverse Flow
Tailpipe	1.88	1.88
BRAKES		
Front—Drum Diameter (in.)	10	11
& Width (in.)	2.5	3
Rear—Drum Diameter (in.)	10	11
& Width (in.)	2.5	2.5 (lining optional)
SUSPENSION		
Front Wheel Rates (lbs. per in.)	120	140
Torsion Bar Diameter (in.)	.88	.92
Sway Bar Diameter (in.)	None (.84 optional)	.94
Rear Wheel Rates (lbs. per in.)	120	170
No. of leafs	4.5	5.5
Front Roll Rate (lbs. per in.)	120	240
Rear Roll Rate (lbs. per in.)	105	145
Shock Absorber Diameter (in.) & Type	1.0 Direct	1.0 (Heavy Duty)
TIRES		
Size	7.35 x 14 except wagon 7.75 on 2-seat wagon 8.25 on 3-seat wagon	7.75 x 14
Type	2-ply Rayon	4-ply Nylon, Low Cord Angle
AXLE		
Rear Gear Diameter (in.)	8.75	8.75, 9.75 w/ 4-speed manual
Ratio—Manual	2.94, 3.23	3.54
Automatic	2.94, 3.23	3.23

SUPER STREET CHEVELLE

ERIC DAHLQUIST
Hot Rod, February 1966

*'66 SS 396—These are the call letters of a spirited new model
from Chevy, designed for those who LIKE to drive*

"Have any trouble keeping it on the ground?" The question came at us through a grey wall of water, which was part of the pre-Thanksgiving deluge that engulfed southern California and put our 396 Chevelle Super Sport test car through a wet set of paces during the 1,000 miles we had it. Our interrogator was everybody's idea of how a young American male should look, outfitted in a yellow Nantucket slicker with a stream of water cascading off the brim. He knew it was a 396 because it said so on the front fender and had those "wiggy" air ducts on the hood. He also wanted to know if we had taken it to the strip yet and how it compared with the 442s and GTOs and how much it cost (because he was going to buy one) and if we had had our parking ticket validated. All this in the middle of a parking lot in a pouring down rain.

Chevrolet has been kind of out of it for the last couple of years, as far as having its own hottest hot dog, but after the parking lot caper, it's apparent that guys still remember when she was real fine, that 409, and how Dyno Don Nicholson and Frank Sanders put 'em back on their heels at the drags in 1961 with their first demonstrations of what a stocker could do. The wave of enthusiasm that the 409 created carried stovebolt maniacs along, and the Beach Boys helped with their dragging ballad ("Giddy-Up 409"). So did the Daytona "Mystery 427," which some of the executives back at the plant still say is a mystery to them as a misty look comes to their eyes with recall of how those '63s set the track on fire.

So this is what it had all boiled down to: the semi-hemi, porcupine top, 4.094 x 3.76-inch 396, like the one *Hot Rod* broke the story on last year, plunked into a 115-inch wheelbase Chevelle with a black vinyl top and a lower body color known as Aztec Bronze, reminiscent of something called Titian Red from the mid-1950s. The two-door hardtop has those "in" for this season "struts" or "sail panels" (or just plain extensions), emphasizing that desirable fastback silhouette from the side, but embodying the practicality of a more vertical, recessed (in relation to the extension) back window. Then, too,

Going or coming, the Chevelle 396 SS stood up to the challenge of the wide country, not losing its footing even on the serpentine mountain trails. Heel-over was contained in marked degree, due mostly to 30 percent stiffer springs and shocks, as well as a fat anti-sway bar.

this negates the manufacture of a special glass piece just for fastbacks, which, considering the volume Chevy sells, makes for a fair budgetary chunk.

Those in the know can spot the 1966 SS 396 from its earlier counterpart because there has been a concerted effort made so that they can. Little changed since it was first introduced in '63, but the new Chevelle has undergone such style transformation as to resemble more closely the full-sized Chevy, which it does, most handsomely. As another play to identification, all the grille bars in the SS have been blacked out except for the top and bottom, which is an inexpensive way that any Chevelle owner can escape the "I'm from Detroit-fluorescent light grating" look. All 396ers come with the red line 7.75x14 NF nylon tires (U.S. Royal) on wide-base six-inch rims. Our test machine also had the benefit of a set of the optional mag-spoke hubcaps which, from anything beyond 20 feet, appear more real than what they're imitating. But probably the easiest way to know that you've just been or are about to be passed by one is by reading the SS 396 signs that are hung on, as is mentioned at the beginning of the story. Since the factory has gone to all this trouble to advertise, the enterprising "Bondish" type will no doubt derive endless hours of delight by swapping his 396 emblems for 327 or, sly dog, 283 counterparts—but that's another story.

After originally announcing last year, with the inception of the new engine, that only about 200 of the 396-equipped Chevelles would be available, quite a good number more than this were run off. Although one of those original was not included in our testing program, we drove a representative sample and found it to be quite interesting although a trifle nose-heavy. In 1966, this negative trait has been cured to a point that even our 360 horsepower version with optional cam (322-degree duration and 0.3983-inch lift compared to 340 and 0.4614) and Muncie four-speed was a totally pleasant vehicle, just the ticket for a quiet Sunday drive or drag. Helping toward this goal are the 30 percent-heavier-than-normal front and rear coil springs, larger-valved shocks, 15/16-inch diameter front sway bar and neat things like front ball joints that are shot-peened to frustrate the development of cracks.

It has been felt in some quarters, especially after breaking an axle, that Chevelle rear housing stabilization left a bit to be desired when it came under hard usage. Now a good part of this deficiency has been rectified. It is also quite obvious that a great deal of attention has been given to the hind quarters in general. To begin with, the stiffer rate rear coil springs and shocks will go a long way toward controlling wheel hop under acceleration or hard braking. In addition, there is a new frame reinforcement strut between each rear upper and lower control arm pivot point, which will solidify the rear section considerably. The axles themselves have a sturdy differential carrier with a big 8.875-inch diameter ring gear, which means, in practical terms, that it is a full 3/4-inch larger than the common run-of-the-line unit.

The axle ratio standard with our 360 horsepower model was 3.73:1 but, unlike some years within easy recall, there is a veritable myriad of gear combinations from which to select. If you go for the baseline 325 model, a 3.31 ratio is standard, with 3.55, 3.73, and 4.10 on the shelf if specified. In 360-land, when the machine is equipped with a three-speed manual, power-glide, or street-type four-speed, the choices are identical to the ones just enumerated. However, should a close-ratio four-holer be beneath-the-boards, you could opt among 3.31, 3.55, 4.10, 4.56, and 4.88—the last three being Positraction as part of the deal. Limited slips can also be had in any of the other gear sets as well. Viewing the whole rear scene in perspective, it looks as though all bases are pretty much covered.

At the other end of the ship, things are not out of shape either. For your motivation, it's an either/or proposition—either the standard 325 pony package or the several-hands-higher 360. That's it—no sixes or smaller eights to muddy up the water or drag down the car's reputation. Just two brands of hair—long and longer. But not quite as long as last year when the rated power pegged out at 375 and the machine had more of a blast effect. Why? Well, superficially at least, the '66 cam timing is less exotic, for one thing. As for the upper-level decision to retrench from last year, one can only guess that the original 396 just didn't fill the bill as a machine that a great number of people would like to be married to for 36 payments. And after all, image or no, this is why the thing is on the market.

We could go into gales of specifications on the 396 engine, but this has already been done in copious form in *Hot Rod*, starting with the original 396 story back in March of '65 and continued varyingly in the recent Bill Thomas and Smokey Yunick pieces. Enough research has been done on the powerplant to answer just about any question of maintenance or modification.

Today's breed of box is identified by the numerical ratio of its first gear, such as 2.52 or 2.20, the latter being most desirable and the former being what our SS came equipped with. These two transmissions are the only four-speeds that are offered with the Chevelle 396, and both are listed as heavy-duty. For the wide-ratio transmission (2.52, 1.88, 1.46, and 1.00), as opposed to the close-ratio (2.20, 1.64, 1.27, 1.00), numerous improvements have found their way into the design. Specifically, the teeth of the clutch gear and meshing member of the counter gear have a coarser pitch for increased durability. In addition, the new counter gear incorporates a damper to virtually eliminate backlash. Both transmissions, wide- and close-ratio, feature a larger diameter counter gear shift and reinforced synchronizer blocker rings.

Another choice heretofore not available in any Chevy product is an all-synchro three-speed. This configuration has now been added to the 396 SS line and, like the four-speeds, is considered a heavy-duty option. With ratios of 2.41, 1.57, and 1.00, it represents a sturdy assembly that incorporates wide, constant-mesh gears. Probably most interesting of all Chevy transmissions is the one which isn't even being offered in the Chevelle line at all—the three-speed Turbo Hydra-Matic. The outfit is decently light and responsive, but for some reason it has been withheld as an option from the "A"-bodied series. We recently had the opportunity to drive a former to-speed Chevelle that had been converted over to Turbo action, and the gain in performance, seemingly at no sacrifice to economy or dependability, is startling. This is one instance where the division is missing a good bet, and with competition being what it is, little will be gained by dallying.

So now that we've surveyed the salient properties that combine to form the character of the SS 396, let's drive the thing to work for a while, bend it into a few corners at speed, ridge-run a mountain road or two, and play an odd hand at the drags. Foremost in our minds, as indicated above, the 396 is an especially nice package to get from point to point and to have a measure of fun while doing it. The 360 horsepower version's 3.73 final drive ratio is a happy compromise in union with the four-speed that you can row along on its Inland shift linkage. Action with the 11-inch centrifugal clutch was generally smooth, but now and again a slight amount of shudder was evident when hot, after stop-and-go driving.

The one area we did get to examine carefully was the adequateness of water sealing. For most of the time the car was ours, the rains came with sickening regularity, day in and day out, to break all records, seasonal or otherwise. During this dampish phase, the car never sprang a leak in spite of many "river crossings" and the two-speed electric wipers could not be faulted. However, something that does need alteration is the brakes, or rather lack of them, judging from their performance after wading through an intersection pond six to eight inches deep in water. It is quite understandable that with a drum-type arrangement, 268.6 square inches worth, in fact, that the binders will tend to become ineffective for a short period, but more than once it was necessary to drag the pedal for several long blocks to dry them out. We put the car on a hoist to survey the situation, and it appears that the shield Chevrolet engineering has devised to keep water out of the drum also serves as a dam to hold it in. In other portions of the water world, like heavy rain or the normal shallow puddles, no problem was encountered.

While the 9.5x2.5 molded asbestos binders are at least equal to the task of everyday traffic, successive stops from over 60 are not their forte as pedal effort increased and the right front wheel (on our car) tended to lock up. Fortunately, there is a cure within the RPO

Almost enough to make a man abandon his horse, this "bonanza" of sleek silhouette styling corrals a stallion's spirit.

list—a nifty set of welded sintered iron brakes that rise to fill the breach. Although we did not have the opportunity to try the iron anchors, several owners reported that this is the way to fly—there is no warmup problem, the things wear forever, and they stop on a dime over and over again without temperamental displays. We inquired further and learned from area dealers that, speaking for southern California, a goodly number of SSs are sold with the metallics, so at least a portion of the buyers are playing it safe for any contingency.

We noted that even in the wet the Chevelle was admirably sure-footed when in traffic, and when the rainmaker did finally close up shop, a definite date was kept on some twisty L. A. County mountain roads. In the first serious encounter, an inordinate amount of tire squeal was produced by the "Tiger-Paws," so we beat it back to the nearest service station to check the air pressure, which turned out to be right on the suggested front specs. But wait—there is a hidden lie in the figures. Recommended settings are always values for cold tires, and as tire heat increases, so does air pressure. We didn't have time to adjust and readjust pressures, so we settled on 28 psi (cold) all around.

As anticipated, the SS lived up to its advance billing and gave a good broken-field demonstration, limited only by tire adhesion. The car would charge into a turn, mild understeer would dissolve to neutral, and then shade to oversteer with the aid of the throttle. The "Tiger-Paws" are good, a measurable cut above the rest of the normal stuff, but there are several shoes, at least two from Europe, that would complement the Chevelle's road manners even more. That nice fellow, the average SS buyer, wouldn't find anything wrong with the Royal Red line because it was superior to his standard of comparison. But the fact of the matter is Pirelli, Michelin, Firestone, and Goodyear have tires for a price that will, under near-impossible conditions, stick like glue.

Of all the things the SS 396 should be, it is competitive at the drags. We dyno tune some of our test vehicles and maybe slip on a set of slicks and/or headers. Just for a change, and because it didn't look too prosperous for a break in the weather, the Chevelle was left in pure condition except that the Holley four-throat with its vacuum-operated secondaries was modified to open properly. For reasons of economy, the vacuum operation of the secondary is retarded by a small coil spring and, often as not, the tension keeps the back butterflies closed until quite late in the acceleration range, or until the vacuum overcomes the resistance of the spring. It was apparent while trying to get away from rest in best fashion without bogging that the engine had to be revved to about three grand. This induced much undesirable wheelspin. So the vacuum diaphragm housing was disassembled and two coils snipped from the spring. Presto! The low-speed power problem was corrected.

After a couple of wet weekends, the skies cleared and we went out to San Fernando Raceway for a half-dozen passes. The day was bright and sunny, but the temperature was down in the low 60s and a 30-miles-per-hour head wind forecast is not the most ideal of racing conditions. Even using extreme caution, the first run produced some wheelspin, reflected in the elapsed time of 16.30 seconds (86 miles per hour). Since traction seemed the major problem, we thought a few of the match racer tricks might be of some help. So the tires were burned through puddles of bleach for super cleaning and some liquid traction compound painted on. This done, the machine recorded a better 15.70 elapsed time at 92 miles per hour. We realized that without the benefit of adequate dragging skins and a proper collector system, you can't expect miracles but the wind and cold track had something to do with it, too. Besides, there was a '65 Chevelle SS with 375 horsepower, NASCAR Holley, slicks, and who knows what else that wasn't going more than a second quicker. His hydraulic lifters were adjusted a little tighter than ours and, therefore, permitted a rev limit about 200 rpm above our 5,500 rpm. We also clipped off some 0 to 60 and 30s with the 3,850-pound hardtop, which at 7.9 and 3.2 seconds respectively, along with the quarter-mile speed, indicates that the potential is there if plumbed properly.

All the time we drove the 396 SS, it drew a great deal of attention from the younger set, who seemed to dig everything about it—especially the simulated hood scoops. Several who looked inside noted the luxurious maroon vinyl upholstery and gauges instead of idiot lights as something worth plunking down $3,800 for. The bucket seats this year feel more straight-backed than previously and generally impart the idea that they provide better support on the sides. Appointments inside were almost all class "A" with a sensible dash layout whose only bad feature was that at night the illuminated tach face cast its reflection dimly into the windshield. We regard with mixed emotions that some of the trim on the dash is now chrome-plated plastic instead of metal, but at least in damp climates it will not rust, and this is some consolation for the cheapening effect.

As a synopsis of the random reflections that ran through our mind as we returned the car to the Chevrolet zone office, it could be said this 396 SS was the type of vehicle we hated to part with. It has just the right measures of ride-handling and acceleration that would make it the nuts for all kinds of driving, especially long trips. It's a fun car for today's dull traffic, and if it helps relieve the tedium of travel, you can't ask much more.

FORD'S FAIRLANE
500 GT/A STYLE

ERIC DAHLQUIST
Hot Rod, March 1966

After a time in other waters, "Dearborn" drops the venerable 390 mill into an improved Fairlane chassis and comes up with a GT series that's apt to make you get in the swim of things

Four wheels and a board make a Ford. That's what they used to say in the northeastern area where we grew up. This terse comment on the talents of old Henry was directed specifically at his Model T and its somewhat stiff riding qualities (this must be some kind of record in owner identification after 20 years) and also to the fact that the car was a pretty simple piece of iron, easily repaired in the bargain.

But this was the voice of the older generation, the people who viewed things from realistic perspectives. To a youngster, it was a horse of a different color. To them, the Ford (almost any Ford) was a car blessed with the mystique of looking just right, somehow more right than anything else on wheels. And faster, too. After all, that's how a lot of us got together under the banner of hot rodders in the first place, isn't it? 'T,' 'A,' '32, '36, '40, '41, '46, '49, you pick 'em. For a lot of years the Ford was the car to have if you were to be considered "in"—a spot where everybody short on years wanted to be.

Unfortunately, the many people who bought Fords usually bought them used because they just didn't have the coins for the new stuff like their older and better-heeled parents. So along about the mid-50s, Ford tried more and more to orient their products toward the people who bought the cars or more specifically, Chevrolet cars. Being No. 2 just didn't get it. So this brings us to 1963 and Ford is still No. 2, but a queer thing has happened. The young set now has a good deal more loot to spend on wheels and there's a lot more of them—like there's a youth market now. So who's built more machines taken to the hearts of the young than anyone else? More important, who's realized what's happened? You guessed it.

Henry smiles wryly from the gloom.

In 1966, Ford really has gotten with the program. We almost knew they would, for after all wasn't the Mustang the fairytale success story of the century, and weren't a lot of Fords being watched going by by the competition? So when the cars were unveiled during the magazine press preview time in Detroit, there was no question that the bunch

Newly styled for 1966, the Fairlane has seemingly recaptured earlier Ford charm.

looked like odds-on favorites, and the Fairlane, ooh wow! A lot of people commented that the Fairlane seemed to bear a resemblance to last year's GTO, but if it did, who cared? Not the customer. By the turn of the year, sales were up 27 percent and No. 2 was almost No. 1.

With all these happenings going on, we were anxious to get our hands on one of the middle-sized Fords for a thorough road test and drag strip evaluation. Of course, not just any Fairlane would do. It had to be the GT/A hardtop (A is for automatic in case you didn't know) with 335 horsepower mill, stiff suspension, and sticky 7.75x15-inch Firestone Super Sport skins plyed on Ford Motor Company's boss mag wheels that are actually steel. Oh, yes! It was a metallic bronze beauty 197 inches from head to toe, 74.1 inches from shoulder to shoulder, and when it slid to a stop in the garage, we were convinced it had to be one of the best looking Fords ever built. Apparently we weren't alone in this judgment for almost everybody gave it the eyeball.

On all of our tests, we try our darndest to drive the machines into road situations similar to what most of you would encounter. However, the one thing we have trouble duplicating is those northeastern-type Currier and Ives winterscapes. This time, fortunately, southern California's low-lying areas had experienced quite a good measure of rain (about 400 percent more than normal in fact), and this meant lots of snow at higher

Chic wheels and a racing stripe below the belt line make this car a hit.

elevations. So, we packed Eric Rickman aboard and headed up the curvaceous Angeles Crest Highway for some time on the slopes.

One of the first things you notice about the interior is its generally good seat-to-steering wheel relation and the fact that the bucket seats don't give sufficient support to the thighs (at least on my six-foot, three-inch frame). The 16-inch steering wheel is extra nice because it's on the small side and, with the help of the 21:1 (29.4:1 for manual) ratioed power assist, will allow easy manipulation as well as entries and exits without getting your legs wedged between the rim and the seat. Besides all this, the tiller is a nylon simulated

In general, the dash and interior are well designed. The off-the-shoulder console and sport-shift are new additions for the '66. The small diameter wheel was easily handled.

wood job that looks equally as good as one of those handcrafted European pieces but is infinitely more practical—it won't dry up and eventually crack. After all, it is embarrassing to have your hand lanced while playing Jim Clark. If you're inclined to such sport, it would no doubt be helpful to know that lock-to-lock requires three and a half revolutions of the wheel and one revolution of the car uses 41.5 feet.

Another interior feature of inestimable value is the T-handle of the three-speed Cruise-O-Matic Sport-Shift that calls the plays for one of the best transmissions with which we have had experience. Ford has gone to great lengths to advertise the versatility

Pop art? No, it's the new emblem of performance in the B/Stock or "youth-market" clan.

of the sport-shift and it lives up to its advanced billing. The unit can be left in drive and will automatically shift through its 2.46:1, 1.46:1, and 1.00:1 ratios or, if the driver desires, be put through its paces manually, up- or down-shifted or held in any gear. This feature really comes into its own on some place like a mountain road where you'd like to get through the bends with "vigah" yet retain precise control: You're in high at 50 and there's a sharp curve ahead. Your hand slips to the T-bar and your thumb presses the black release button in and click— the "Cruise-Os" in second and the engine's braking. As the car begins to lean slightly to the outboard side on the 300-pounds-per-inch rate front coils and 105 pounds-per-inch rear leafs (normal is 220 and 78 pounds-per-inch, respectively), you see that a little power can be applied because the car is really giving it that "on rails" try—and there it is, right on tap and hot.

Pushing the Fairlane brought two things to light: the vehicle is a very rigid platform, which comes through tight curves with a one-piece feeling; additionally, the boys back at engineering have done their suspension homework. The underbody of this machine is what might be termed a "neo-unit" in that there are front, rear, and side rails joined together with torque-boxes and crossmembers. Welded to the side rail structure is the reinforced floorpan that has the familiar driveshaft tunnel hump that, besides providing an occasional obstruction to rear passenger movement, acts as sort of a full length backbone for extra rigidity. The torque-boxes are areas where noise and vibration generated by the suspension, engine, and driveline components are absorbed before they can be relayed to the passenger compartment.

Because of the torque-boxes role, they have been designed to allow a certain amount of flex to absorb secondary shocks and road irregularities. Despite the seeming contradiction between rigidity and flexibility, the concept works admirably well in keeping the passengers isolated from not only a rough ride but also fatigue-inducing noise while allowing as solid a car as you'd like. The heavy-duty suspension is no doubt largely responsible for this fact and helps to explain the reason why even sports cars of a considerably higher price bracket will be hard-put to leave the Fairlane flatfooted in any situation.

If you've seen Ford's "quiet man" on TV, moseying about the European landscape challenging various famous marques to match an upstart American vehicle in lowness of noise level, then the natural inclination is to expect parallel standards in the rest of the line, which includes the high-performance Fairlane GT series. And we've got to admit that they've done a good job of it, sealing out the rest of the world. All over the car there was graphic evidence that sound deadening material abounded. On every car we test, we like to punch in the headliner with a finger and see if there's anything up there between it and the roof except air. On a good share of today's iron, the only thing to be found in the roof cove is that emptiness that produces that steel drum–concert effect. But not in the Fairlane. There's a one-half-inch blanket of fiberglass to wrap you in silence, and even the vertical roof pillars are filled. Under the floor mats, hood, rear seats, inner fender housings, wherever you care to delve, someone's been there before you putting on fiberglass or deadeners of one kind or other.

And as this stuffing keeps the noise out, it also wards off the cold wind's breath in winter and allows a shirt sleeve environment with the assist of a heating unit that belts out the BTUs in copious amounts. It wasn't really too chilly the day we went scaling in the mountains, somewhere in the lower 20s, but nonetheless, the heating plant was appreciated for its efficiency.

With the 4,000-foot level came the white stuff, and most of the road from there on up was cloaked with a sheet of hard-packed snow, glazed in some spots. Despite this, the Fairlane demonstrated that it would stick to the track without the use of snow tires or chains. For photography, we pulled off several times to park and found that accumulations of about four inches was all the traction factor would stand before a moderate amount of wheelspin developed trying to get away from rest. Having spent more than two decades facing the white deluges of the Northeast, we would hazard an educated guess that a good set of snow tires will get the car through most situations. Balance is pretty good.

Another spot where the GT/A showed that it was light on its feet was on the dry sections of the twisty asphalt we were on. You can drive hard into even the tightest corner with confidence that the Fairlane's behavior will remain predictable. There was very little noticeable understeer and in most instances the altitude was one of neutralness (with little lean) that changed to oversteer as the accelerator was depressed. As we pressed through this day with verve, the only discouraging points were that the bucket seat just didn't get the job done providing sufficient support while providing over-sufficient firmness, and secondly, for some reason the speaker in the radio gave forth with only fuzzy notes although station power seemed satisfactory. Since we have heard the quality tones of other Ford audio units, it seems evident that a new speaker would have provided the cure.

Winding our way back down the llama's path, we let the power-assisted brakes assume the load, rather than the transmission, to see if this part of the package could stand shoulder to shoulder with the rest. GT models come standard with 10x2.5-inch drum brakes both front and rear, providing a total swept area of 314 square inches. This compares favorably with other 390 and 289-ci Fairlanes that offer 282.6 square inches of swept drum

HOW TO COOK A TIGER

Take one part 335 HP V-8. Chrome plate the rocker covers, oil filler cap, radiator cap, air cleaner cover and dip stick.

Blend high lift cam; bigger carburetor.

Mix in the new 2-way, 3-speed GTA Sport Shift that you can use either manually or let shift itself.

Place the new shift selector between great bucket seats.

Now put on competition type springs and shocks.

Add a heavy-duty stabilizer bar.

Place over low profile 7.75 nylon whitewalls.

Touch off with distinctive GTA medallion and contrasting racing stripe.

Cover with hardtop or 5-ply vinyl convertible top with glass rear window. Serve in any of 15 colors.

This is the new Fairlane GTA. An original Ford recipe that may be tasted at your Ford Dealers . . . Remember--it's a very hot dish!

FAIRLANE

GTA

A PRODUCT OF Ford

An ad promoting the 1966 Ford Fairlane GT/A.

area. There was no mention on our spec sheet of anything other than common asbestos for lining material, but whatever the composition, it got the job done—stop after hard stop required little or no increase in pedal effort. We tried a series of rapid halts in succession from 60 miles per hour, and there was no sign of uneven pulling or unexpected lockup. It is our opinion that the Fairlane's GT brakes complement the car nicely and despite the fact a few people would prefer discs, the additional help really isn't needed.

Over the years since Ford introduced its 390-ci engine (with 4.00x3.78-inch bore and stroke), the company has had generally good luck with the unit because it has always been capable of getting the job done in excellent no-complaint fashion when asked to do so. A quick glance over the powerplant's salient character shows the development of a remarkable 427 pounds-per-feet of torque at 2,800 rpm. This has got to be one of the highest figures in the hot medium-compact class and not only previewed good drag strip potential but overall muscle. Noteworthy too was the fact that maximum horsepower was derived at 4,600 rpm, meaning that the hydraulic lifters are good at least this far without pump up. Although our car didn't have a tach, in actual practice we guess that the lifters will grab almost a grand more on the .440-inch lift cam without difficulty.

This is welcome evidence that Ford has finally seen the light as far as producing high-performance cars without easily pumped lifters that put a strangling noose around the horse's neck. In the past, many a young man bought a four speed–equipped Ford with a set of 4.11s in the rear only to find that the lifters were done lifting at 3,800 or so rpm.

Another spot where the cars are looking good is in the carburetion department. Instead of avoiding the issue, Ford has stepped up to be counted with a 2818 Holley, which will be appreciated by the racers due to its good power-producing capabilities. Of the many test machines that have had vacuum-operated secondaries on their carbs, this is the only one that has worked acceptably to date. We think Ford realizes that the potential GT customer is not transfixed with the notion of passing more gas stations than competitors, so they gave them what they wanted.

One thing that did fuss us a bit in the engine compartment was that the single point distributor was retained instead of an excellent dual-breaker sparker produced for some of the other models and that is now a drop-in item. (For those who might want to drop one in themselves, the part number is COAF 12127K). We're not mentioning what we consider a deficiency just to be knit-pickers or because it gave us much concern when readjusting its point gap every once in a while; it's just that if you want a reliable performer, this particular single-pointer is not the answer.

When we went out to San Fernando Raceway, we anticipated that our GT/A would bear good account of itself, despite the fact it had the stock 3.50:1 axle ratio, no slicks, headers, or dyno tune job. The only things done to the Fairlane were to check to see that the butterflies were opening completely and set the float levels in the carburetors, an adjustment made externally on a Holley. With a power rating of 350 horsepower and a shipping weight of 2,821 pounds (3,486 pounds curb weight), the GT/A falls solidly into C/SA, the most popular class at the drags. With GTOs, 442s, Gran Sports, Skylarks, Chevy 396s, and other hot-house varieties residing in this patch, it makes for very spirited rivalry indeed.

After a series of familiarization passes, it became evident that the sport-shift worked best when operated manually, and in so doing, we got a 15.70 elapsed time at 92 miles per hour flat. Acknowledging the fact that this wasn't the hottest time ever turned didn't dampen our enthusiasm because we had the class' top time and low elapsed time for the day. Later on, we learned of another 1966 390 that ran a bunch of 14.20s at 98 miles per hour by merely adding a 4.11 final ratio and slicks.

And we wouldn't doubt this a bit because that torque output translates into dig you can't believe, especially after the second shift. Going toward the traps, the Holley throats gulp down cubic feet of air that won't quit, and the engine sounds as if it will accelerate forever. Once you try it, you've just got to do it again. It's great!

Perhaps this last sentiment characterizes the Fairlane GT/A as appropriately as any. It's a hard charger but not a hard rider or a hard master when it comes to the price tab— which isn't bad at $3,279, as tested. In fact, it's pretty darn good as prices go in this area. With this you'll get the power seating, power brakes, "wheels," automatic, radio, etc., plus elicit comments like this one we received from a parking attendant at a swank restaurant: "Fairlane . . . since when did Ford start building neat cars like this?" It looks like they're back at the same old stand. Move that Model T over.

FIREBIRD

ERIC DAHLQUIST
Hot Rod, February 1967

Hark! I bring you glad tidings of great joy: Supercars are out, super-supercars are in. This, along with the micro-skirt (replacing the miniskirt, which was obviously fated for short-lived popularity), will set 1967 down as a watershed in American automobiles. How dare we be so prophetic? Easy, chum, if you've just driven down to General Motors proving grounds in Mesa, Arizona, and seen the Firebird.

"The what bird?"

"The F-i-r-e-b-i-r-d, friend." Remember that name. It's one species of Pontiac you may regret "fouling" around with.

Last year, old No. 3 pumped 100,000 GTOs out of the well into the youth market, 100,000 fresh-faced American youngsters who wanted immorality for 13 seconds – that's not asking much. You'd have thought the chief, John DeLorean, would have been happy, but he didn't get that little silver number in his lapel for complacency. No, he got it for walking softly and carrying out things like the GTO, SOHC six, and understanding what it's like to be young.

So he watched Chevy bring out its Camaro, John DeLorean did, and then he grabbed the body configuration for Pontiac (but that's all) because he knew there was a Cougar and a Mustang already on the trail, and he wanted to show what can done even when you're only No. 3. Small things. Like redesigning the Camaro's frustrating radio knobs so that they're still safety contoured but easily to manipulate. And offering a B. F. Goodrich-conceived inflatable spare tire right out of tomorrow-land that let you use more reasonable the limited trunk space, not to mention showing your friends how the crazy thing inflates to a regular 14-inch two-ply and then shrinks right back to about one inch larger than the rim when the freon is let out. It's like that bald Erasian that keeps popping in and out of Mr. Clean bottles.

Big things. Like a 400-inch GTO-type powerplant sitting in there bold as brass and a 1-2-3-speed Turbo Hydra-Matic transmission behind it. And behind that is the biggest

Swoops and dives form the Firebird's sleek hood toward its divided-grille. The 400's twin scoops can be made functional to vent in cool air.

full-sized GTO axle you ever saw. Remember how the unaided Camaro had the single-leaf spring that hippety-hopped to the barber shop and then some? Well, the Firebird's still got just two one-leafers back there, but it hasn't got two cents worth or wrapup because right below those two spring bands are a pair of the neatest traction bars. Maybe they shouldn't even be called traction bars since they appear more like miniature Funny Car lift bars, yet they pivot at both ends. But don't go away; there's one more gimmick you drag guys will flip over. The Firebird's traction arms incorporate an adjustable positive stop, making it easy to change the degree of leading to suit strip conditions. You see, Mr. DeLorean really cares.

Nobody's kidding anyone else, you know. The 390 Mustangs and Cougars were the first super-super voileys, the 350 Camaro the second, and then the 383 Barracuda. It didn't take any great amount of genius to know that Ford would be easily handing in there with a 428 option like Carroll Shelby's got right this minute on his 500 GTs or that the Camaro would have anything else but a 396 (with Nickey dropping 427s in as fast as their hot little chain-falls would recycle). So Pontiac had the 400 (325 horsepower) engine in mind all along, and maybe the 428 if things get hairy. Even the so-called Ram-Air package is there for the x-ing of the appropriate slot on the order form. Other considerations might be: 400 V-8, 318 horsepower @ 4,800 rpm; 326 V-8, 285 horsepower @

Voila! Pontiac starts with a 400-inch top-line power choice right off the bat. The engine can be GTO duplicate right down to Ram-Air package if you want.

And this is the trick of the decade—a seemingly mild-mannered puny circle of rubber that puffs to a mighty 14-incher. The tube holds a freon cylinder.

5,000 rpm; 326 V-8, 250 horsepower @ 4,600, 230 OHC 6, 215 horsepower @ 5,200 rpm, 230 OHC 6, 165 horsepower @ 4,700 rpm.

Right off the bat we expected that the 400 Firebird ought to be a short-fused GTO and then some. After all, our test Camaro went into the high-14s with only a 350-inch powerplant and those 4.3 inches of length that Pontiac styling added on the front couldn't make that much difference.

And away-y-y we go. Pontiac engineer Trevor Brown and *Hot Rod*'s Eric Dahlquist cruise for a hot quarter-mile.

Well, it wasn't just the extra sheet metal, it was a little bit of this and a little bit of that and the bright red prototype convertible sagged in at 3,855 pounds . . . not to mention a copilot to slog our running weight past two tons! That it ran as quick as 15.4 and as fast as 92 miles per hour is remarkable, since the car had been previously flogged quite a bit. With those big Firestone wide ovals biting in, the Firebird whistles off the mark and there's no way you can get on iota of wheelhop. Give us the "air-cooled" 400 machine down around 3,400 pounds and we'll take on the world.

We stole a 100 mile-per-hour lap on the endless five-mile banked oval and the Firebird was as solid as a reindeer stock on Christmas Eve. The car most certainly feels stiffer that the Camaro (probably due, in part, to the Firestones) and also demonstrated a greater tendency to understeer in sharp radiused curves because of the additional engine weight. By contrast, the SOHC six we tried, if on the sluggish side a low end owing to an improperly calibrated Quadrajet carburetor, presented a very well-balanced arrangement otherwise. Pontiac is the only American company that has gone out of its way to glamorize the six, and it's a real shame that the others haven't followed this lead since most modern, light inlines are better-handling crates than the lordly eights.

It's a funny thing, but when Mercury uncaged its Cougar, the car shared the same basic body with Mustang, but you'd never know it. Pontiac, apparently less prone to

1967 FIREBIRD

PRICE
As tested . . . . .N/A

ENGINE
Cylinders 8
Bore and stroke 4.120x3.47
Displacement . . . . .400 ci
Compression ratio . . . . .10.75 to 1
Maximum horsepower . . . . .325 @ 5,200
Maximum torque . . . . .410 @ 3,200
Valves:
   Intake . . . . .2.113 in.
   Exhaust . . . . .1.773 in.
Camshaft:
   Lift: . . . . .413 intake, 413 exhaust
   Duration . . . . .301° intake, 313° exhaust
Carburetion . . . . .Single 4-barrel
Exhaust system . . . . .Dual

TRANSMISSION
Type . . . . .Turbo Hydra-Matic
Ratios: 1st . . . . .2.48 to 1
             2nd . . . . .1.48 to 1
             3rd . . . . .1.00 to 1

DIFFERENTIAL
Type . . . . .Semifloating
Ring gear diameter . . . . .8.125 in.
Ratio . . . . .3.08 to 1

BRAKES
Type . . . . .Delco-Moraine disc front;
                                                        drum rear

SUSPENSION
Front . . . . .Independent
Rear . . . . .Single leaf spring

PERFORMANCE
0–30 . . . . .2.5 sec.
0–45 . . . . .4.7 sec.
0–60 . . . . .7.5 sec.
Standing quarter-mile . . . . .15.4 sec at 92 mph

DIMENSIONS
Wheelbase . . . . .108.1 in.
Overall height . . . . .51.6 in.
Overall width . . . . .72.6 in.
Overall length . . . . .188.4 in.
Curb weight 3,855
Test weight 3,855
Crankcase capacity . . . . .5 qt.
Fuel tank . . . . .18.5 gallon

shoot the works on a big body bill or just less solid on the idea, came up with a divided grille bumper configuration that some angles betray as an add-on afterthought. The Firebird 400's beautiful twin-scoop hood really deserves a more sophisticated frontal assault. So does the obviously good suspension engineering.

A trial flight of 50,000 'Birds will wing their way to American highways, and if the demand is phenomenal, this figure will be escalated and possibly a more enterprising variation hurried out next year. It is not anywhere as unique a vehicle as the GTO was, and the marketing boys to not see it eating into their loyal 100,000 buyers. And maybe this is the whole deal: Pontiac wants a car to snipe at the Cougar but not at the GTO's expense. It's a status thing for the older guys, you see. Besides, those micro-skirts just go so far.

FOUR OF A KIND

ERIC DAHLQUIST
Hot Rod, April 1967

Come with me Lucille and get clued-in on the hot setup for the supercar sweepstakes—Olds for '67; what a way to go

In 1957, Tommy Hamilton had it all. He was the king of strip and street because he drove an Olds. Not just an ordinary Olds, but a '50 Club Coupe with a '57 J-2 Tri-power. It was one of the first supercars, and if you lived and loved fast machinery in western New York a decade ago, you remember that formidable Cad/La Salle shift lever sprouting erect as a metal pine from the floorboard and the way the car won B/Gas in the days when you could still relate to drag racing.

And that's the way it was, brother; Olds was the hot tip. There were those Rocket V-8s with their never-say-die bottom ends, beefy parts that just went on forever shutting off the world, and whoever heard of a GTO? Out there in California, Gene Adams was building a legend around himself with a blown '50 fastback—and remember the Olds-powered Ratican-Jackson-Stearns Fiat A/Altered, or when Lenny Harris won the Nationals in '60 with the beautiful Albertson Olds rail? Those were the last golden moments of the fabulous '50s, when Oldsmobile men looked down their noses at the triflings of other marques who fought to keep pace with the innovator.

Then this brilliance from Lansing, Michigan, was suddenly blotted out by a great cloud of garish, chrome-draped mediocrity that drove away the enthusiasts at a time when the youth market was being born, and you didn't especially want to do that. In fact, Olds blew a decade-and-a-half advantage. But there were those who remembered the good old days, so when something was needed to stave off the GTO, these men created the 442. Boy, we loved that first car—mostly because it was such a fleet road runner, and then it reminded us of that brick-commode construction of previous vintage years, too. But the kids didn't buy it; at least not like they might have. Solidarity meant extra weight, which meant slower elapsed times, which meant no deal. That was until last summer, when Olds announced a tri-carb manifold in combination with a W-30 cold-air induction package plus slightly redesigned heads and won C/Stock at the nationals. Holy cow, they were back!

As '67 loomed, it looked as if the 442 would put it on everybody; the car was pretty good looking to start with, the engine was proven, and the tri-power was putting out the ponies like you wouldn't believe. But then the head office came down hard on multiple carburetion in A-bodied cars after the safety row, so the jugs went flying off to a premature retirement and a single Quadrajet was it. Even so, the 442 seemed a good bet and feelers were put out for a possible test. Jim Williams at Olds PR did us one better, offering an alternate idea: take four of their specialized intermediates, three 442s (a stick, an automatic, and an all-out B/Stocker) plus the "engineer's special," which has since become known as the Turnpike Cruiser, and let the people know what the division has to offer in variety for the enthusiast. Since GM and its affiliate divisions are officially out of racing, Hurst-Campbell's performance

Among the cars tested were the 442 four-speed, 442 the automatic, and the Turnpike Cruiser, kind of a detuned 442 with Puritan overtones only in the gas department.

division in Detroit was selected to prepare a competitive B/Stocker with legal blueprinted 400-inch powerplant and chassis setup that included a running weight of 3,400 pounds. So propositioned with what anybody in his right mind would call the racer's dream, first the production machines and then the B/S filtered into our provinces. Both showroom 442s were a sight to behold: 115-inch wheelbase rafts of speed lavished with smooth acrylic lacquer. The standard-shift job was a brilliant Spanish red with black vinyl roof and the automatic was a dazzler Olds calls saffron but everybody else called yellow: a yellow set off with a red pin stripe and red-line Firestone wide-ovals that people just gawked at till it was out of sight. And when they looked inside at the matching vinyl interior floored with brown deep-pile carpeting, they—even L. A.'s jaded teeny-boppers—blew their collective minds. Boy, is Olds missing the boat on this one. Why not a fleet of eye stoppers spotted in selected metropolitan areas around the country to attract buyers? The *coup de grace* was the rump-rump cold-air pack cam in the automatic, which sounded like a Riverside L.P. and just so mean that you didn't have to race anybody.

But the 442 is no put-on. From the special reinforced frame to the all-Olds-beef 31-spline rear axle (8.75-inch ring gear, 32 percent more strength) to fore (.937-inch) and aft (.875-inch) sway bars, the car means business. Where the GTO has always been able to more than acquit itself on the straightaway, the '65 442 showed superiority in winding road-course situations, and the '67 is even better. Back at the long-lead preview, the Olds people sat us down and presented, among other things, a first-rate seminar on handling and controllability (by D. E. Condon) that let people know that the whole business was a sophisticated problem and that sophisticated approaches were used to solve it. There may be a few flaws in the 442 as far as handling and controllability go, but it's hard to spot them. In almost all situations, the car is basically neutral and therefore a joy to drive, especially in the presence of most foreign-born contemporaries on a twisting road.

Not that the general public is any more interested in this than they are in fastening their seatbelts, but if the time ever comes, Olds will have a lot of points. Right now, the thing is straight-line performance; if you've got the best off-the-showroom runner, you win. The catch is the off-the-showroom clause. Kids today don't want to fool with a finicky powerplant, no matter how hot it's supposed to be when in perfect tune. Gas, oil, and plugs are about the extent of it. And this is where the 442 shines.

Even equipped with stock gearing, the stick (3.42) and Turbo Hydra-Matic (3.08) felt good on the street, but a trip to Irwindale Raceway was an eye-opener. Both cars had initial runs in the 15:50s and 60s with everything as is. As previously mentioned, the automatic had the cold-air performance camshaft, but factory engineers considered this a liability rather than an asset since the rear-end ratio was not in the range to allow quick rpm. The power-steering belts were removed completely and the alternator ones loosened for a tenth, but the real gain showed up when the gas tanks were filled (extra ballast) and the rear tires pumped to 32 pounds (55 front). Wow! 14.70s. About this time, Tom Churchill, the strip's B/Pure Stock record holder happened by with his 442 (3.90 gear) and suggested removing the detent arm from the carburetor's air valve to the dash pot, which would eliminate the momentary lag in throttle response common to the Quadrajet. This was good for a little more, and coupled with adjusting the distributor (9 degrees initial, 36 degrees total) until slight ping occurred just after the traps at full throttle, produced a 14.57–97.50-mile-per-hour run in the automatic and a fantastic 14.38–100 for the stick. Even more impressive was the fact that both cars had under 900 miles on the odometer. Equally important, although the stick had a good .2 quicker elapsed time, the automatic wound up the winner by a hair in four straight runs—ah, the disadvantages of natural selection.

But were we satisfied with this? Well, for a little while, and then we started thinking about a 4.33 gear, slicks, and the rest of the cold-air pack goodies. By this time, the Hurst expeditionary crew (Bob Riggle, Dick Chrysler, later augmented by Paul Phelps) had arrived (a few days prior to NHRA's Winternationals) to add the special parts and deliver the prepared B/S to Century Olds in Van Nuys, who was to campaign it. The automatic 442 already had the cold-air cam and heads, so the only thing the boys had to do was slap on new heads, relocate the battery in the trunk, put a new axle in (4.33), install a "trick" (higher-shift-point) automatic to complement the cam's long-rev characteristics, put in some red plastic lightweight inner fender panels, fit the air ducting, and add a set of air lifts to the back to help jack weight. That's all. On the standard shift car, the new cam was added, plus this other stuff.

Out at Irwindale again, we quickly learned that the factory-engineered combination in stock form was extremely well coordinated. Where the Firestone wide-ovals had been adequate before, now they spun as if on ice and the elapsed times for both machines were only a tenth or so better than before. Bill Casler happened to be out at the track himself that day (he had generously rented the facility for two days during the week prior to Pomona to allow anyone who wished a chance to tune before the big meet. How's that for good will?), and he came up with a pair of seven-inch-wide slicks (29-inch diameter) that were admittedly too tall even for 4.33s but were slipped on anyway because that's all we had. Using all the rpm on the line available (1,800–2,000 with brakes locked) gave the automatic about two dozen runs in the low 14s, varying from 14.19 to one "everything's-just-right-and-feeling-so-fine" 13.97 with speeds in the 97 to 99 range.

The four-speed was an even better story. A standard shift's major attraction has always been having the full rev band at your disposal to suit differing track conditions, so with the big tire we just brought the engine up to about 4,300 and let it happen—13.92-104—about equivalent (for an unblueprinted, 3,710-pound sedan practically strangled by closed exhausts) to winning Indy on stock tires.

While the street jobs were making about a jillion runs, the all-out racer was cooperating by first breaking the spot welds where the axle tubes and the third-member housing mate and then, once this was fixed, shelling the teeth on the pinion gear like hasn't been seen since the corn was ripe in Iowa. The trouble was that giant 9.50x15 Goodyear boots just put too much footprint on the track. "But just a minute, wise guy. If those new Olds rear ends are so big and strong like you just said, how come they're breaking?"

"We'll bet you remember old campaign promises, too." The deal is this: Olds doesn't make its own ratios past 3.90:1, so all the rest of the choices higher than this are carried over from Chevy. Even though the Stovebolt stuff is just about able to hold its own in a lighter machine, under a heavy Olds, the situation really gets grim. The unit-setup for living 4.56s and others like that is a Perfection Gear pinion (30A4062B), and then you'll be able to do sweet things like 12.61 at 110.42 miles per hour, just like George DeLorean (Hurst's regular engine man) in the hot job. 'Taint bad, McGee.

As the last strip session concluded, there was that nagging realization that when you start changing combinations on a car you usually affect one and probably many other things along with it. You put in the good dragging gear ratios and suddenly the stock tires have gone south in efficiency. But even slicks aren't the whole answer because now the car feels lazy out of the chute as the rpm is down and the W-30 cam doesn't work right at low speed with closed exhaust. And then if you went the open header route, the carb would go lean, and when this was right the tires would probably be off again, and it's a vicious circle. The fact of the matter is that the production 442 is an example of compatible, interrelated, superior engineering that is successful by itself.

Nobody has ever been able to build a good performance economy car in America before, but Olds has come through with their Turnpike Cruiser, evidence that the innovators are on the march again. Shelby 350 GTs notwithstanding, it is probably this country's first GT car built not by European standards, which for some reason are almost always blithely applied out of context to nearly totally different environments, but to prevailing Yankee requirements. Like we've got the best system of highways in the world, right? But they are not anything like those of Europe, so the type of vehicle built for them must be different, too. Right? Oldsmobile engineering thought it was high time for someone to offer a fast, safe, good-handling machine for today's limited-access thoroughfares that would not kill you with high-engine speed vibration or finish you off at the gas pumps with more stops than a Greyhound.

Actually, the TC is a lot like the 442 automatic (400-inch powerplant, stiffer suspension, quicker steering, stronger frame), but with the substitution of radial-ply tires, 2.41 drive ratios, and a two-barrel carburetor. Because of the 2.41 gear, right away you can see the long-legged potential, but what about that two-bore jug? That can't be good for snap, can it? Well, it can because of the good low-speed torque characteristics of the 300-horsepower engine and the Turbo Hydra-Matic's flexibility. Would you believe that the car's elapsed time is only half a second slower than the stock 442 with 3.08 gear and four-barrel (15.50s compared to 16.00-16.17s)? And in the economy run it won hands down, never falling below 18 miles per gallon and sometimes reaching 21—shades of the 6s. Because of the great turbo, the car is fun if not surprising in city traffic and it sails down those long open roads.

Of course, it shares a few of the 442's basic faults. The dashboard is contemporary Mickey Mouse, falling far short of the handsome GTO layout, which truly conveys the idea of an automobile. The rev counter is too small, jammed into the same nacelle with the clock, oil pressure, and amp gauges, and if this hash allowed the ad boys to call it a tick-tock-tach, then the whole bit is a joke anyway. A wide, flat hood races out ahead of the driver, but the wide expanse of slightly reinforced metal invites flutter even on California's glass-like roads. Wind noise was at a surprisingly low level in all the cars, not because of the closeness of any interior door fit, but rather because the rubber stripping did a splendid sealing job.

And then there is that so-called "sail-pillar" styling in the back that gave styling an almost fastback profile without a lot of the cost because the normal back window was retained and the rear quarters extended past it. Well fine, guys, but you can lose a small Mayflower van in the blind spot. We're suggesting another outside mirror to complement the one on the driver's side (adjustable from the inside, we might add). Braking on all the cars was way above average, but the disc-equipped 442s just seemed a better idea than the all-drum police specials on the Turnpike. All units were power-assisted, but the discs were more willing to get the car down from speed, and with less effort at that. The TC drum solo is final proof that Olds is not fooling around with the gas economy bit because disc-brake drum drag can cost you a few pints and Lansing wants none of that. Same goes for the wide-ovals on the 442s, compared with the Turnpike Cruiser's Uni-Royal radial plys, which didn't ride as well, much less corner better. We know that radials will give better mileage (both gas and tire) and are probably the safest because high-speed heat buildup is not a problem, but things like a Jello-y feedback through the rear end on some types of bumps shows that the tires and the suspension need a little more adjusting to be happy.

Obviously a great deal of care had been taken in predelivery preparation, for the cars were right—free from all the knobs that fall off, doors that don't close, trunks that fit funny, and exhaust rattle-type annoyances that can literally drive you to distraction. The standard-shift machine suffered the only disaster of the street jobs in losing one header pipe bolt and a bushing in its otherwise slick-working Hurst shifter (that doesn't tele-graph that old Muncie-wind sound of former days because of total rubber isolation). Century Olds personnel took particular pains to demonstrate that they not only service what they sell but do it right the first time, a fact that makes the division sure of repeat customers if all its outlets are like this.

Our test cars were just bags of fun to drive in both stock and slightly mod form, each possessing particular endearing qualities that made selecting one above another difficult. The four-speed is kind of a nice old-time touch, but the automatic can be manually shifted and is just as good; who needs the extra hassle of going up and down the gears in modern, congested traffic? Unique in its own right is the Turnpike Cruiser,

Make: Oldsmobile Blueprint Spec.
Power Team or Option No. 360 Horsepower 442 (W-30)
Model Year: 1967
Date Released to Public: December 9, 1966

ENGINE:
Type & No. of Cyl.: 90° V-8
Valve Arr.: Overhead
Bore: 4.00
Stroke: 3.975
Displacement: 400 ci
Compression Ratio:
   Nominal: 10.50:1
   Maximum: 11.00:1
Maximum BHP: 360 @ 5,400
Maximum Torque: 435 @ 3,600
Cylinder Head Vol.: 71.9 cc min.
Head Gasket
Thickness & Vol.: .023–.027 5.34943 cc min.
Deck Cl. & Block Vol.: .002 min. 2.0604 cc min.
Total Comb. Chamber Vol.: 79.30983 cc min.
Minimum combustion chamber volume may not
exceed the maximum compression ratio.
Min. Deck Clearance: .002 below
(Specify above or below block)
Give engine identification
numbers and location: Prefix V
        Stamped R.F. cylinder head
Approximate weight of complete engine, as installed,
with all accessories—but without flywheel, clutch,
and clutch housing. 644# (Dry)

PISTONS:
Description: (Flat, Dished,
Dome Head, etc.): Flat Head
Displacement of Dish or Dome: ....ccs

CYLINDER HEAD
Part No.: 387174 or 389213
Cast No.: 389395 or 383821

INDUCTION:
Number & Type: 4-barrel carburetor
Make: Rochester
Model w/S.M. Trans.: 4 MV
Model w/Auto. Trans.: 4 MV
Part No. w/S.M. Trans.: 7027156
Part No. w/Auto. Trans.: 7027156
Power Team or Option No.: 360 ci
Camshaft Part No.: 397329
Lifter Type: Mech   Hyd X
Model Year: 1967
Camshaft Casting No.: 389410
Rocker Arm Ratio: 1.6:1

TIMING:	**INTAKE**	**EXHAUST**
Checking Clearance		
Opens (BTC) (BBC)	44° BTC	90° BBL
Closes (ABC) (ATC)	84° ABC	38° ATC
Overlap	82°	82°
Duration	308°	308°

VALVES:		
Head Diameter(Max.)	2.067	1.629
Angle of Seat & Face	30° Seat	45° Seat
	and face	and face
Lift (Max.)	.474	.474

SPRINGS: With inner dampers		
Outer Valve Closed	84	84
(Max.)	@ 1.670	@ 1.670
Outer Valve Open	194	194
(Max.)	@ 1.270	@ 1.270

kind of a detuned 442 with Puritan overtones only in the gas department. If you live at or near the track, then the B/Stocker is a good choice for rapid transit.

About the only drawback these cars possessed were rather steep sticker prices of between $4,500–$5,000. All that lush interior stuff, the tilt column, electric windows, and seat are nice, but the Turnpike Cruiser had nearly two grand's worth of options and that's got to be stretching things. We suppose you could say that fabulous gas mileage saves enough to pay for the options, but the average buyer will pare the price down to a more realistic $3,500. People serious about knocking off GTOs don't need excess baggage. Besides, those good old '50 Olds coupes didn't have any fat on 'em, they were all business—the business of being king.

Make: **Oldsmobile Blueprint Spec.**
Power Team or Option No. **350 Horspower 442**
Model Year: **1967**
Date Released to Public: **December 9, 1966**

ENGINE:

Type & No. of Cyl.: **V-8 90°**
Valve Arr.: **Overhead**
Bore: **4.00**
Stroke: **3.975**
Displacement: **400**
Compression Ratio:
    Nominal: **10.50:1**
  Maximum: **10.93:1**
Maximum BHP: **350 @ 5,000**
Maximum Torque: **440 @ 3,600**
Head Gasket
Thickness & Vol.: **.023-.027 5.34943 cc min.**
Deck Cl. & Block Vol.: **82.40983 cc min.**
Total Comb. Chamber Vol.: **82.40983 cc min.**
Minimum Combustion Chamber Volume may not
exceed the Maximum Compression Ratio.
Min. Deck Clearance: **.002 Below**
(Specify above or below block)
Give engine identification
numbers and location: **Prefix V**
Stamped R.F. cylinder head
Approximate weight of complete engine, as installed,
with all accessories—but without flywheel, clutch
and clutch housing. **.637# (Dry)**

PISTONS:

Description: (Flat, Dished,
Dome Head, etc.): **Flat**
Displacement of Dish or Dome: ....**ccs**

CYLINDER HEAD

Part No.: **394500**
Cast No.: **394497**

INDUCTION:

Number & Type: **4-barrel carburetor**
Make: **Rochester**
Model w/S.M. Trans.: **4 MV**
Model w/Auto. Trans.: **4 MV**
Part No. w/S.M. Trans.: **7027036**
Part No. w/Auto. Trans.: **7027036**
Intake man. Casting No.: **390390**
Power Team or Option No.: **400 ci**
Camshaft Part No. **393854-SMT**   **396193-AMT**
Lifter Type: **Mech**   *Hyd*   **X**
Model Year: **1967**
Camshaft Casting No.: **396189**
Rocker Arm Ratio: **1.6:1**

TIMING:

	INTAKE	EXHAUST	
		ATM	STM
Checking Clearance		0	0
Opens (BTC) (BBC)	30°	71°	78°
Closes (ABC) (ATC)	76°	31°	28°
Overlap	58°	52°	58°
Duration	286°	282°	286°

VALVES:

Head Diameter (Max.)	2.067–2.057	1.629–1.619
Angle of Seat & Face	30° Seat	46° Seat
	30° Face	45° Face
Lift (Max.)	.472	.472

SPRINGS: *With inner dampers*

Outer Valve Closed	76–84	76–84
(Max.)	@ 1.670	@ 1.670
Outer Valve Open	180–194	180–194
(Max.)	@ 1.270	@ 1.270

VEHICLE	Olds 442 (Stick shift)	Olds 442 (Automatic)	Olds Turnpike Cruiser
PRICE			
As tested	$4,523.49	$4,760.46	4,944.52
ENGINE			
Cylinders	8	8	8
Bore and stroke	4.00x3.975	4.00x3.975	4.00x3.975
Displacement	400 ci	400 ci	400 ci

Compression ratio	10.5 to 1	10.5 to 1	10.5 to 1
Maximum horsepower	350 @ 5,000 rpm	350 @ 5,000 rpm	300 @ 4,600 rpm
Maximum torque	440 @ 3,600 rpm	440 @ 3,600 rpm	425 @ 3,000 rpm
Valves: Intake	2.057 in	2.057 in	2.057 in.
Exhaust	1.619 in	1.619 in	1.619 in.
Camshaft: Lift	.472 intake, .432 exhaust	.430 intake .472 exhaust	
Duration	282°	286°	
Carburetion	1 4-barrel Rochester Quadrajet	1 4-barrel Quadrajet 1	2-barrel Rochester
Exhaust system	2.25-in. exhaust pipe 2.00-in. tailpipe	2.25-in. exhaust pipe 2.00-in. tailpipe	2.25-in. exhaust pipe, 2.00-in. tailpipe

TRANSMISSION

Type	Standard 4-speed	Automatic 3-speed Turbo	Automatic 3-speed Turbo Hydra-Matic
Ratios: 1st	2.52	2.48	2.48
2nd	1.88	1.48	1.48
3rd	1.46	1.00	1.00
4th	1.00	N/A	N/A

DIFFERENTIAL

Type	Salisbury limited slip	Salisbury limited slip	Salisbury limited slip
Ring gear diameter	8.75 in	8.75 in	8.50 in.
Ratio	3.42 to 1	3.08 to 1	2.41 to 1

BRAKES

Type	Delco-Moraine disc front, drum rear	Delco-Moraine disc front, drum rear	Duo-Servo
Dimensions: Front	11.00 in	11.00 in.	9.50
Rear	9.50 in	9.50 in	9.50
Swept area	348.4 in	348.4 in	291.0 in.

SUSPENSION

Front	Independent, coil spring	Independent, coil spring	Independent, coil spring
Rear	4-link, coil spring	4-link, coil spring	4-link, coil spring
Stabilizer	Front, .937-in.; rear 8.75 diameter	Front, .937-in.; rear .875 diameter	Front, .937-in.; rear, .875-in. diameter
Tires	F-70x14 Firestone wide ovals	F-70 Firestone wide ovals	195 R14 Uni-Royal radial ply
Rims	6-in. wide	6-in. wide	6-in. wide
Steering gear: type	Power	Power	Power
Ratio	26.7 to 1	20.7 to 1	20.7 to 1
Turning circle	41.7 ft.	41.7 ft.	41.7 ft.
Turns of steering wheel, lock to lock	4.06	4.06	4.06

PERFORMANCE

Standing quarter-mile	100 mph in 48 sec. 104 mph in 13.92 sec* *with W-30 "cold air" package, 4.33 rear-axle ration, and 7-inch slicks)	97.1 mph in 14.50 sec., 99 mph in 13.97 sec. * * with W-30 "cold air" package, 4.33 rear-end ratio, 7-inch-wide slicks	85 mph in 16.6 sec.
			0.30 ... 3.2 sec.
			0.40 ... 5.1 sec.
			0.50 ... 6.2 sec.
			0.60 ... 8.7 sec.

DIMENSION

Wheelbase	115 in	115 in	115 in.
Front track	58 in	58 in	58 in.
Rear track	59 in	59 in	59 in.
Overall height	54.5 in	54.5 in	54.5 in.
Overall width	75.4 in	75.4 in	75.4 in.
Overall length	204.2 in	204.2 in	204.2 in.
Curb weight	3,630	3,630	3,630
Test weight	3,710	3,700	3,900
Crankcase capacity	4 qt.	4 qt.	4 qt.
Cooling system	16.2 qt.	16.2 qt.	16.2 qt.
Fuel tank	20 gal.	20 gal.	20 gal.

BEEP! BEEP!

ERIC DAHLQUIST
Hot Rod, November 1967

For fast, fast, fast relief from option misery and high-price distress, take a Road Runner. Look! What is it? I dunno. Beep-Beep! It's the Road Runner

The 3/4-ton flatbed truck had just bounced out of a dusty tomato field onto the narrow two-lane highway east of Albany, New York. The three teenagers riding in back were stripped to the waist, work gloves tucked in their belts, and skins burnished to a deep tan from hours under the sun. Their shoulders slumped a little from the day's labor.

Then they spotted us, and their world of dust, sun, and tomatoes compressed to a gunmetal gray machine with a black vinyl top. It was like nothing they'd ever seen before because it was a '68, and the '68s weren't supposed to be out for four more weeks. Beep-Beep! But they knew the horn. It was the sound of the Road Runner, and the Road Runner is what's happening.

The kids, millions of 'em, sit in front of their TVs every Saturday morning and watch the bird and coyote have at it in living color while the old man rides around the grass on his Lawn Boy or stokes the charcoal broiler. The kids turn on, tune in, and drop out of that white collar jazz. They couldn't care less about the four-door sedan sitting out in the driveway—the car they're supposed to wash. Who needs it? It's a beige metal box to get back and forth from ulcer-land with. Right? So it's reliable; so's a Checker cab.

Chrysler people were the squarest dudes in the world when it came to the delinquents putting down their iron, but the company finally understood that out there in that sea of fidgeting juveniles spilling Kool-Aid and popcorn on Mom's new carpet were, among other things, potential customers. In fact, most of the customers they were ever going to have for the next 20 years or so.

So now the joint starts jumping a little, and things like the street hemi come along, but that isn't the answer, either. It's too serious—about as funny as Uncle Joe Stalin—and it's been done, kind of. The kids are pretty much all fed up with the dumb real world, anyway; it's not their bag. What is? Obviously, the GTO.

"You know what's wrong with the GTO?" says a voice from the far end of the board room.

Tastefully void of ornamentation, this machine is as clean in style and price as a kid could want. And you'd better believe that the kids will want it because car's complete as is, with nothing to buy, no hidden fees, or clauses. Just slide into a local Plymouth showroom, put down the coins, and go have a ball.

"What?" asks another.

"It's too expensive by the time you get everything on it you want. Money, now that's a serious matter. Why don't we bring out a new kind of car that has everything on it to start with? A package of fun with stiff suspension, big brakes, goer-type engine, hood scoops, and a reasonably low tab. And just so nobody will get mad when we beat them, we'll put on a beep-beep horn like the Road Runner—in fact, let's call it the Road Runner. It'll cost us an arm and a leg to get Warner Brothers to go along, but think of the merchandising possibilities. Anyway, there isn't a GT or XR that hasn't been used already."

It takes a lot of elan to do something like Chrysler did (use a cartoon character to set the theme for a new car), and it also takes a fair amount to start off on a cross-country road test with a car showing only 6.9 miles on the odometer, but if Chrysler was game, so were we. Besides, we weren't going all the way across the country, just from Detroit, Michigan, to New York City. What could happen?

Feature Editor Dahlquist? No, it's his brother Charlie, who specializes in making Corvairs run back in the old hometown (Lockport, N.Y.), but he dialed into Road Runner electrical shortcomings in nothing flat anyway. "Looks like a winner," Charlie's terse comment on machine, was re-echoed by the guys out at Madison Township drags even before it ran.

THE PLYMOUTH
road runner

© WARNER BROS. PICTURES INC.

And that, pal, is what Road Runners are made of. It's a supercar in every sense of the term but one—price. That's why you're going to love it. The accessories, a very few like the hemi, are there, but the basic package will blow the doors off almost anything in the asphalt jungle and some of these cats cost a grand more. You can do a lot with that extra thousand dollars. The old man will like it.

A lot. The mere fact of tooling around the public roads with the absolute first production anything, let alone a boss machine, creates almost as many disasters as a miniskirt on a motorcycle. Hardly had we cleared the guardhouse at Chrysler's Lynch Road assembly plant when the first guy wanted to know what it was. Beep-Beep. Any more questions? Besides the horn, our 'Runner had the 325-horsepower 383 engine with 440 heads, cam, intake and exhaust manifolds, heavy-duty street hemi suspension, 3.55 Sure-Grip rear end and four-speed transmission outfitted with an Inland shifter. And, of course, Goodyear wide-boots on Kelsey-Hayes wheels—a supercar's got to have super wheels, right?

If you know anything about this part of the country, you understand the plan is to shortcut through Ontario, Canada, to either Niagara Falls or Buffalo, New York, and then grab the thruway for the city. Everything was just dandy until about five minutes after the people at Chrysler called it a day and went home; that's when the sky fell in on us. Without warning, the ammeter began indicating a 40-amp charge condition, and when we pulled into a service area to check it out, an alarmingly steady stream of water began leaking from the cross-threaded petcock. Since this particular garage had no instruments to check out the alternator, and we learned that the radiator did not leak when the engine was running (in fact, it never leaked again once it was refilled),

Out at the drag strip that looks like all drag strips should, Madison Township, our first production Road Runner went like all Road Runners should—fast: 98 miles per hour in 14.74 seconds with 850-odd miles on it. We knew it would go better and it did. How about 102 in 13.98? No cold-air kits or trick cams or blueprint jobs, just stock with a few more hours down the road. And that's another thing. It's good at going down the road—hilly or flat, straight or hairpin—the RR's got as much balance as the Bolshoi Ballet.

there was no alternative but to press on regardless, draining off as much excess electricity as possible with the accessories and headlights.

Back on the road once again, things progressed happily until, in a little town called Paris, about 70 miles from the U.S. border, the engine went utterly dead. On the face of it, the symptoms indicated that the gas tank might be dry, but after a quick examination, this diagnosis was switched in favor of no electricity to the coil. All the wires seemed properly plugged in, but with no working light available, much less any tools, and still no current, we hot-wired a direct lead from the battery to the battery side of the coil and headed for our brother Charlie's automotive repair shop that happens to be conveniently located a few miles east of Niagara Falls, New York. Bright and early the next morning, it took the two of us about 15 minutes to trace the difficulty to the firewall junction block where the wires from the engine compartment connect with those under the dash. Externally, everything looked fine, but inside, the hot lead from the ignition switch was separated just sufficiently to break connection. This could have happened because someone goofed on the line, or because the firewall flexed under certain conditions, or just from vibration.

Once more we headed east toward N.Y.C. (actually Staten Island), where we had scheduled an F-85 Olds V-8 into Corvair engine swap story, plus a few passes at the closest strip. Everything was hanging in there just right as the miles clicked off and the engine loosened up. Since the Road Runner is aimed at a low relative price range (as supercars go), the interior is intended to be neat but not what one would call lavish, being executed in flat black-and-gray vinyl with a firm but comfortable bench-type seat. The one thing that bugged us was the gauges, which, although they were thankfully not idiot lights (except oil pressure), failed to create the same kind of gutsy, precise feeling as a GTO. The tachometer, for example, is over on the far right of the instrument cluster, and besides being out of the driver's direct line of vision, lags about 500 rpm behind actual engine speed during quick acceleration.

When we finally landed at Art Silva's pad (the guy who had the V-8 Corvair), our road test crew was suddenly swelled by not only Art, but also by enthusiasts Jack Johnson and Dennis Samuelson, a group ready as anything to zoom through the forests of Staten Island and out to the Madison Township Dragstrip at Englishtown, New Jersey, in the first Road Runner.

To say that it rains quite a bit in these parts is the understatement of the year, and of course the Sunday we went out to the track provided maritime scenes to rival Sir Francis Chichester's circumnavigation of the globe. This brought to light an interesting situation: On a damp, rainy day, with four people in the car, the windows fog over immediately, which means you turn on the defroster, which is so efficient that it reminds you of those hot-air hand dryers, which means you put down the windows for some ventilation. Fine, but the top of the '68 B-bodied Plymouths (from which the Road Runner was sired) slope in so much (the tumblehome factor, as it is known in the trade) that rain falls straight into the car when it's moving under 30. It's like those keen GI helmets we grew to know and love, scientifically designed to direct any and all precipitation immediately down your neck. Later on, we learned from one of those keen types in domestic product planning that either we had improperly adjusted the controls (proper adjustment would have allowed demisting without opening the windows) or the controls were improperly connected in the first place. We tend to think it may be the latter, since the possible control settings four people can come up with in three hours trapped in hopelessly snarled traffic during a New Jersey monsoon boggles the imagination.

All right, the interior is on the stark side. But nobody complained about it, just the bogus gauges and that riot-stick Inland shifter, which provides about as much control as a worn-out girdle and is about as effective. Remember swing-out rear quarter windows? Only it isn't a '49 Merc anymore; it's how to keep the price-gap, baby. Would you believe GTO swing-outs for '69?

Despite this minor or major aggravation, depending on how hard the rain is falling, the hearty 383 lugged through river crossings. About the brakes, we couldn't say the same. With a front disc/rear drum combination, the front binders at least dried quickly after each fording, but soon the appropriate red warning light came on because the pedal began to sink to the floor. We had sprung a leak in reverse; the left front wheel cylinder commenced to lose fluid. Since it seems unlikely that the water crossing could have had anything to do with this, we wrote the problem off as an improperly assembled wheel cylinder.

Usually, when you load four adults into almost any American machine, its handling characteristics deteriorate by about an equal factor. But not the Road Runner. The thing

Usually, when you load four adults into almost any American machine, its handling characteristics deteriorate by about an equal factor. But not the Road Runner.

that amazed us most was that even at speed, over what Staten Islanders loosely described as improved roads, the car refused to bottom or flounder. A devoted Sting Ray owner had to admit that the car's adhesive credentials were pretty impressive, and for power steering it did provide excellent road feel. The following day, when Madison track manager Vincent Napp set up the lights for us, we found the acceleration qualities of Road Runner matched its cornering potential.

The car has 325 ponies. Right? And it weighs in at 3,750 pounds with a full tank of gas. Right? And it has a 3.55 rear, the tires don't get hold of the ground on the line, and the Inland shifter is for the birds, but it still made it into the 14s after a few passes. Right? Now let it cool down and put in some new J10Y Champions and—zip—98 in 14.74. Got that? Eight hundred fifty-nine miles on the speedometer and it goes 98 miles per hour. If you know anything about drag racing, you know 14.74 with a 98 mile-per-hour trap speed means the car is being slid off the line to avoid breaking loose. Jacking around tires should get the elapsed time to about 14.30 with a 98 miles per hour. Think of a 3.90 gear, a Hurst shifter, and about a thousand more miles on the car. Try 101–103 at about 13.95. That's fantastic for a showroom stocker. So is 98 at 14.74.

Now the sun was shining brightly, there was a hint of fall in the leaves of the trees that dot the track, which looks more like a park, and we were all standing around with Vince Napp at the starting line, talking about how the Road Runner was going to start a whole new breed of cars to match a whole new generation of buyers and how Pontiac

PRICE
Package price . . . . $2,913. F.O.B. Detroit

ENGINE
Cylinders 8
Bore and stroke 4.25x3.38
Displacement . . . . .383 ci
Compression ratio . . . . .10.5 to 1
Maximum horsepower . . . . .335 @ 5,200 rpm
Maximum torque . . . . .425 @ 3,400 rpm
Valves:
    Intake . . . . .2.08 in.
    Exhaust . . . . .1.74 in.
Camshaft:
    Lift . . . . .450 intake, .465 exhaust
    Duration . . . . .276° intake, 292° exhaust
Carburetion . . . . .1 Carter 4-barrel
    (with air valve secondary)
Exhaust system . . . . .2.50-in. exhaust pipe,
    2.25-in. tailpipe

TRANSMISSION
Type . . . . .4-speed standard
Ratios: 1st 2.66:1
    2nd 1.91:1
    3rd 1.39:1
    4th 1.00:1

DIFFERENTIAL
Type . . . . .Semifloating
Ring gear diameter .8.75 in.
Ratio . . . . .3.55 to 1

BRAKES
Type . . . . .Disc front, drum rear
Dimensions: Front .11.04 in.
    Rear . . . . .10.00x2.5 in.
Swept area . . . . .387.8 in.

SUSPENSION
Front . . . . .torsion bar
Rear . . . . .parallel leaf spring
Stabilizer . . . . .94-in. diameter
Tires . . . . .Goodyear F-70x14
Rims . . . . .5.5-in. wide
Steering gear:
    Type . . . . .Power, recirculating ball
    Ratio . . . . .18.8 to 1
    Turning circle . . . . .40.6 ft.
    Turns of steering wheel,
      lock to lock 3.5

PERFORMANCE
0–30 . . . . .2.1 sec.
0–45 . . . . .3.4 sec.
0–60 . . . . .6.2 sec.
Standing quarter-mile . . . . .98 miles per hour in 14.74 sec.

DIMENSIONS
Wheelbase . . . . .116 in.
Overall height . . . . .53.1 in.
Overall width . . . . .76.4 in.
Overall length . . . . .202.7 in.
Curb weight 3,570
Test weight 3,750
Crankcase capacity .5 qt.
Cooling system . . . . .17 qt.
Fuel tank . . . . .19 gal.

was going to have to start scratching. Sure, our test job had a few things wrong with it, but that seems to be one of the occupational hazards of the car evaluation game. Last year, if you remember, we picked up the first 383 Barracuda, started out from Detroit with equally low mileage and made it to L. A. through rain, mud, snow, and sleet with nary a hangup.

Failures or not, poor instrumentation or whatever, the Road Runner is as tight as Jack Benny, and baby, you'd better believe this car will run. Listed among the few options available are a 440 wedge and, of course, the 426 hemi. We'd be perfectly happy to take our chances with that end-all-worlds 383. There is some serious talk that a cold-air induction package will be on the books soon, and we can't even imagine what that will be like. So, kiddies, let the old man have his Lawn Boy and his new Fury III every year and keep watching the tube every Saturday morning, or Madison Township, or even Lions.

FORD'S ULTIMATE SUPERCARS

ERIC DAHLQUIST
Hot Rod, November 1967

 *Circle your choice in the box provided and return to: Mr. Henry Ford II, Dearborn, Michigan 48121. It may be the only way*

Whective we got to Providence, it was a day later than anyone expected so the original scheduling went all to pot. But Tasca Ford is still impressive. There are, for example, probably more Shelby GTs here than anywhere outside Shelby's chain-link fenced-in corner of the Los Angeles International Airport. Performance Manager Dean Gregson showed us through the shop area where mechanics (the likes of John Healy, who gives his undivided attention to keeping the Tasca Mystery Mustang in the 7s) hone the rolling stock to perfection, through the showrooms where a legion of salesmen make what must be the best deals in the country, through the conference room upstairs where those same salesmen man a battery of phones once a month to make sure the honeymoon isn't over with the customers, and into Bob Tasca's office, which surveys a sight to gladden Dearborn's heart—a veritable sea of multicolored Ford roofs in the lot outside.

Bestriding all of this, like the Colossus of Rhodes, was the character of the "Big Bopper" himself, Bob Tasca.

"You'll get the real story of the operation when Mr. Tasca gets back from Detroit," Dean, as well as everyone else, told us—over and over again until we began to expect some kind of superman—a Wizard of Oz who could wave his magic wand and make everything beautiful. Funny thing about it, they were right.

The original idea for going to Tasca, more or less, was to do a feature on a progressive, performance-oriented dealer. So Dean got out the scrapbooks and told us how it all began back in 1962 with a 406 Ford Tudor that had shoe polish lettering, went 13.19, and was hardly ever beaten. Then, more years of winning, with hardly a loss: an A/FX with Bill Lawton at Pomona '65, 221 wins in a row with stock-bodied cars by July of the same year—and through it all, the giant shadow of Bob Tasca.

And then, unknowingly, we began to hear the hottest scoop of the year.

"We sold a lot 390 Mustangs last fall and into the winter, but by March they dropped off to practically nothing. That's when the snow melted off the asphalt."

With a little help from Bob Tasca and the performance team at his dealership, this power-boosted Mustang is ready to roll.

Soberly, Dean went on. "In fact, we found the car so noncompetitive for the supercar field, in a sense we began to feel we were cheating the customer. He was paying for what he saw advertised in all the magazines as a fast car but that's not what he was getting. So we did something about it. We began to offer the customer little packages of stock pieces to make his machine like it was supposed to be."

The next morning the "Big Bopper" happened. We couldn't have imagined it; it was like standing under Niagara Falls—a ceaseless, overwhelming torrent of ideas, directions, facts, figures, percentages, and analyses. We were walking alongside him, getting part of the story, grasping some of its significance. "The 390 Mustang, even the new 428, isn't competitive with the 400 Firebird, GTO, 442 Olds, Buick Special Gran Sport, Plymouth GTX, Dodge R/T, 383 Barracuda." We were getting into an eggshell-white four-door T-Bird. "You know how many high-performance vehicles (over 300 horsepower) were sold in this country in 1966? 634,434. Do you know how much Ford Motor Company had of this market? 7.5 percent. That's shameful for a 'Total Performance' company."

We sat down in a coffee shop, John Healy alongside me and Bob Tasca across the table with Dean, and we were drinking something called coffee-milk.

The "Big Bopper" himself, Bob Tasca, holds up shots of an earlier project, a restyled-the-way-they-should-have-been-in-the-first-place T-bird. Tasca continually prods honchos at Dearborn to rise above themselves and build machines that are the hot setup. He must be doing something right; he's the world's second largest Ford dealer in the nation's smallest state.

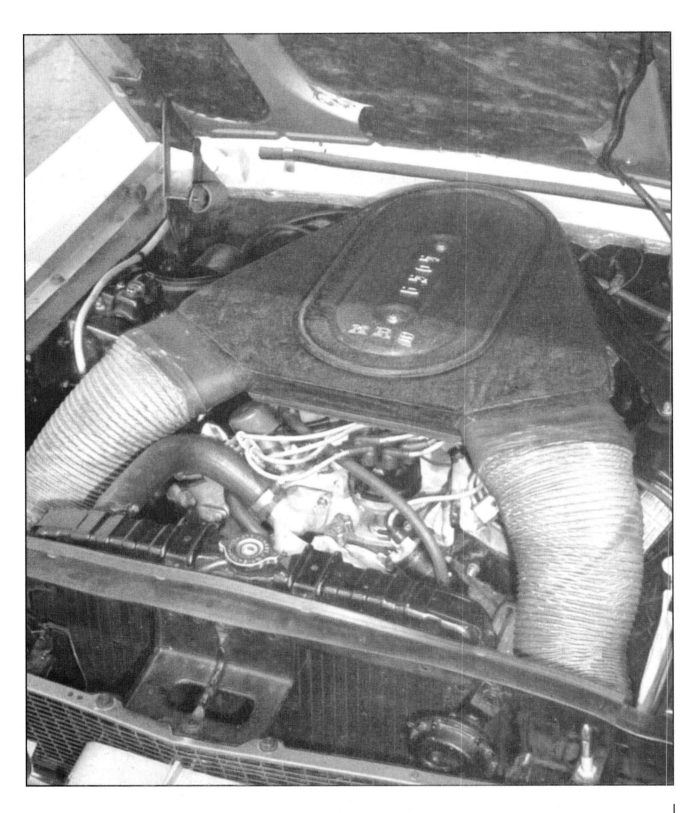

We don't know where it came from either, but somehow Tasca popped up with Lloyd Ruby's Le Mans engine—tunnel-ports and all. The preliminary test program on '69 KR package is already under way.

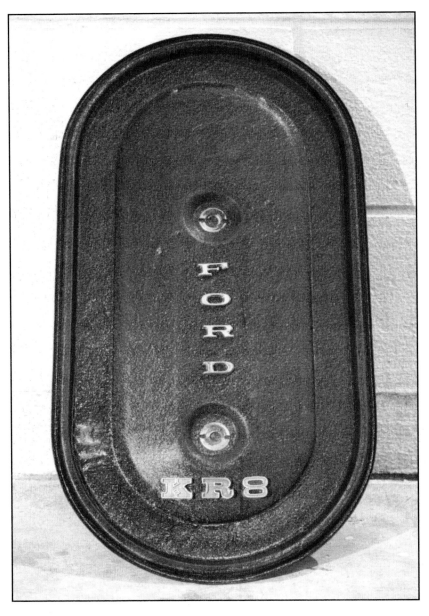

Ford couldn't have made it look more official.

"We can't even sell limited-slip differentials. 11.7 percent of GM units had them in '66, 10.3 percent for Chrysler, and 9.5 percent for the industry. Ford? 5.2 percent. How can we? They don't work."

Now it came along—how Tasca started offering stock performance pieces to augment the 390 Mustang's and Fairlane's sluggish performance. A simple thing like a 3/8-inch gas line to replace the 5/16-inch one, a filter to match (B7T-9155A) and a better fuel pump (COAZ-9350C) for a quick 600 rpm. A more complicated thing like a 427 distributor (C5AZ-12127E), 10-degree plate, 2–3 degrees of advance at 600 distributor rpm, 5–6 degrees at 1,200, 10 degrees at 1,600, 18 degrees lead on the pulley, 32 ounces of point tension, 33 degrees of total dwell, new spark plug cables (C5AZ-12259C), and finally, 1963 1/2 427 heads (C8AE-6049K 68cc) with 2.090-inch intakes (C3AZ-6057J) and 1.66-inch exhausts (C3AZ-6505E).

"Do you know what our 390 Mustang has for exhaust valves? Exactly a 1.566-inch diameter. The 396 Camaro has 1.725-inch diameter units. If it takes big valves to make a NASCAR engine go, it takes big valves to make a stocker go.

"The best cam we could find for all-around performance, especially in the mid-range, was one we already had—the '67 GT/A 390 hydraulic (C6OZ-6250B). By using the 1.76:1 427 adjustable rockers in place of the 1.73:1 standards, you gain .009-inch more lift (an increase in rocker arm ratio of .0003-inch) and, by tightening the adjustment down until it stops clacking, then giving it approximately three-quarters of a turn more, you have 270 degree duration."

The next step was inevitable after the "Big Bopper" saw the '68 Ford lineup and specifications.

"The '68 looked like more of the '67s poor performance, but worse because the cars were heavier. We had to do something about it."

That something was just an entirely new prototype Mustang using most of the parts listed previously, the main difference being a completely stock 428 short-block with 390

Besides wedging suspension for more bite, all leaves on springs are reversed, save the main ones.

cam 3 degree advanced. The chassis was completely tuned for dragging: the battery was located in the right rear of the trunk and it had 427 Fairlane headers, 2-1/4-inch o.d. '66 Fairlane exhaust pipes, 2 1/4-inch Advance mufflers, C-6 automatic transmission (6,400 rpm 1–2 shift, 6,200 rpm 3–4 shift), a deep-sump oil pan, and a cold-air package feeding a Le Mans-type Holley four-barrel carburetor. Manifolding varied but was finally narrowed to a C6H Police Interceptor two-throttle bore configuration converted to four separate throttle bores using a Bakelite spacer that Tasca sells for 60 cents. The spacer allows better direction of the intake charge, preventing some of the fuel particles from dropping out of suspension.

Even though Ford supplied much of the information and pieces for the KR-8 package (as it came to be known), Tasca realized there would be a certain amount of resistance to an outsider's bold ideas. So he did the only logical thing Bob Tasca would do—go right to the biggest bopper of them all, Henry Ford II.

"I told him I believed our cars were competitive in price, more than competitive in style and interior appointments, but hopelessly inadequate under the hood. We haven't

FORD 'HAPPENING' CHART

Engine—Stock 428 Police Interceptor short-block (untouched out of crate)
Heads—1963 1/2, C8AE-6049K, 68 cc per chamber
Valves—Intake 2.090-inch (C3AZ-6057J); exhaust 1.66-inch (C3AZ-6505E)
Valve springs—427, installed at 1.82-inch
Camshaft—1967, 390 GTA, C60Z-6250B (or SK-33222) installed with 3° advance
Intake manifold—Aluminum, Police Interceptor C6H with four-hole Bakelite spacer
Distributor—427 dual-point, centrifugal, C5AZ-12127E, 10° advance plate, 18° lead on pulley, 33° total dwell, 32 oz. point tension
Spark plug cables—C5AZ-12259C
Spark plugs—Autolite BF-32
Transmission—C-6 automatic with heavy-duty convertor
Rear axle—3.50:1 limited slip (28-tooth axles), alternate ratios: 3.00, 3.80, 4.10, 4.57
Fuel system—3/8-inch gas line (replaces 5/16-inch) fuel pump C0AZ-9350C, filler B7T-9155A, 652 cfm Holley carburetor
Exhaust system—1966, 427 Fairlane manifolds, 2 1/4-inch Fairlane exhaust pipes, 2 1/4-inch Fairlane tailpipes
Lubrication system—427 oil pump, 6-quart, deep-sump oil pan (to be replaced with windage tray)
Chassis—Reworked to relocate 40 pounds left rear weight bias to 40 pounds right rear bias. Front 5/16-inch spacer under left front spring pad, increase left front stabilizer link by 3/4-inch, right front by 3/8-inch. Rear: Lengthen right rear spring hanger by 2 inches, left rear 1 inch. Reverse all spring leaves 180° except main leaf and clamp. Install Shelby spring snubbers same as GT-500, Autolite Superflex shock absorbers. Battery located in right rear of trunk (low voltage drop cable)

been the hottest since the flathead V-8 and that was his father's idea so I couldn't congratulate him for that."

Immediately a proclamation for all the nobles from the various departmental fiefs to qualify these assertions went out from the "glass castle." What Henry found out was what every kid in America already knew and that Tasca's KR-8 (which he just happened to have in the staging lane) was quick: 13.39–105.05—with street tires and an efficient (but closed) exhaust. Production 428 Mustangs, Comets, and Cougars should live so long! In fact they didn't against a GTO and Ram Air Firebird. Then the KR-8 dropped both Indians by almost a second.

The question at the moment, lo these many years, was why didn't production performance Fords live up to their advertised image? But it's not that simple. Ford is a big company and in big companies responsibility seeps into many bureau drawers. No person can give the complete, final answer. The bitter irony is that Ford has all the pieces in its inventory (a fact demonstrated by Tasca) to create the hottest volume production machine ever built. It has the talent to put it together and the racing program to fully exploit it, but the myriad of people who pull the strings, the men without whose word nothing moves, are so intoxicated by track victories like dual Le Mans (back-to-back) that they cannot comprehend their street products as being counterfeit. Then too, used to the floating grandeur of an LTD or Continental, the occasional encounter with a Mustang GT must feel like a Saturn V booster. This in concert with what must be a regiment of pie-in-the-sky, silver-lined public relations people, trying their best to shout down the "yes men," must figure in a never-never-land atmosphere.

But enough water over the dam, what everyone wants to know now is what's going to happen. About the middle of August, Bob Tasca hoped the KR-8 package, or some name close to that, would be released in Mustangs and Fairlanes by January 1, 1968. Executives at Ford, when questioned a few days later, at first denied any knowledge and then, when confronted with the facts, admitted a package was under consideration. In engineering, the boys were less than ecstatic. For one thing, if such a GTO-type car did come forth, the ad guys wanted to do something neat like put a 380 horsepower rating on it, enough to guarantee a bad class at the drags and an astronomic insurance factor. Beyond that, some of the warranty boys were yelling, and beyond that there was the strike.

It would be our utmost pleasure to report a low 13-second, 105 quarter-mile machine in street tires and exhaust, ready to pick up at your dealer for the Winternationals, but the project is still in limbo as a regular order piece. For a time, the people at Chevy, Pontiac, Olds, Chrysler, and—clap your ears—American Motors held its

Tasca's hopped-up performance men, Performance Manager Dean Gregson (left) and Assistant Parts Manager Glenn Tiberiis, discuss some of the pieces that are easily available from Ford to make their cars go.

breath, but that's mostly over. "We wondered," said one GM engineer openly, "if Ford ever will get the connection between track victories and showroom sales."

So, unless there's a big scramble, if you want a Dearborn world beater, a bunch of circumstances are going to mean you either build it yourself (from the numbers afforded you here) or buy it from Tasca. By the way he's already working on the '69 version. Would you believe 12.50-110? Absolutely stock.

AN AMERICAN DREAM

ERIC DAHLQUIST
Hot Rod, December 1967

The game is never over until the gun sounds. Hold that thought.
Then, look at the Javelin

They come running down this alley and smash open the gate in the chain-link fence. The fence sounds like the epitome of every chain-link fence that has ever been violated. They spot the car and dash across the street. One of them grabs the bumper, another pops the hood, and still another initiates the classic ritual of siphoning the gas from the tank with a gravity feed hose. The one in the black leather jacket, the leader, stands in the foreground—part of two worlds—giving the orders and acting as a narrator for the audience. Suddenly from the door of one of the nondescript brownstones in the background, a large figure emerges—John Henry in an undershirt. "Beat it, punks!" he booms and the sneaker-shod feet pad into the wings.

It is a microcosm of *West Side Story* and *Our Town*. The Jefferson Airplane and Thornton Wilder. It is a Javelin ad. It is Mary Wells and her gang—Wells-Rich-Greene—doing for American Motors what they did for Benson & Hedges. America adapts!

If fun-type, put-down, clever advertising sells cars, American Motors ought to be striding on the vault at the end of the rainbow. Look at Volkswagen. Yes, do look at Volkswagen. If AM products relate to their ads in a similar manner, everything's going to be all right. The Javelin is No. 4's front runner and it carries all their eggs. From visual impact, we judge it does an admirable job.

Production Javelins were in short supply in September so we got an SST prototype instead. It looked the same but had a number of built-in flaws, which the zone office carefully apologized for ahead of time. Flaws or not, practically no one in those first days had anything but praise for the jaunty lines because they represented an alternative to the rest of the personal car pack. Especially the front end—that massive bumper, floating grille—somehow all those Dick Teague lines just couldn't be from American Motors. Not the American Motors we used to know.

At 109 inches, the Javelin's wheelbase is one inch longer than that of the Mustang, Camaro, and Firebird, two shorter than that of the Cougar. But overall, it's as long as the

The Javelin's massive bumper and floating grille is not typical for American Motors.

Cougar and this makes it five inches more than either Mustang or Camaro. Better yet, it has more interior room than anyone except Barracuda, which is in kind of a class by itself in that it is built on the same size floor layout as a regular-sized compact, and American doesn't want to get caught in an unfair comparison. The Javelin's trunk volume of 10.2 cubic feet offers one more cubic foot of storage than the Mustang notchback and two more than the Camaro. If they offered B. F. Goodrich's Space-Saver spare, they'd gain more volume yet, and then there's always roof-racks, even trunk-racks.

When you get in a Javelin for the first time, several things immediately assault the senses. The seat is surprisingly soft compared to most domestic offerings because American still uses coil construction like Cadillac and Mercedes-Benz. Since the car is equipped with a seat recliner and adjustable steering wheel, just about any driver dimension can be incorporated. Wouldn't you know it though, the vehicle with a good selection of seat-to-wheel choices has an almost perfect setup with its woodgrain sports tiller at the normal angle. This, with more legroom to begin with, is going to raise a lot of questions from owners of other "sports cars" as to why small old AM has a better space layout.

Rear seat legroom provision is measurably better than any of the others, too, but with male passengers back there, an audible clunk is still noted upon hard acceleration. It is the passengers' heads - hitting the back light molding. So, with all the extra

American Motors has shot its Javelin into the air; the carmaker hopes it will land in the general vicinity of the pot at the end of the rainbow. From almost any aspect, Dick Teague's design is fresh and uncluttered, but not controversial—that's important. There are other points, too, like the lever-action door handles—clever, safe, beautiful— in style and in function. The interior, by contrast, was a mixed bag. The legroom in front was great, so were the seats. Instrumentation was adequate but not of GTO caliber.

inches of legroom, the rear seat is still relegated to unbouffanted girl-type secretaries and kids because the head room isn't much better.

Another thing some passengers complained of is the "blah" character of the injection-molded dash, which is probably a tribute, at least in part, to Ralph Nader and the safety people. It does seem, though, that if stylist Dick Teague could create the surprisingly good looking exterior, a little less anonymous dash could have been offered that would still provide crash protection. We guess there's just one bunch, Pontiac, that can come up with a tough job like the GTO and not get the ball lost in the process. Women tend to notice things like this and they also noticed that the seats are high enough and the hood sloped enough to really get a good view of where they were going—and they liked it.

The first car we had with flow-through ventilation was a Saab. And I'll tell you, friend, it worked. The Javelin has flow-through ventilation too, but it doesn't function quite as well, at least not in southern California where, more

Underneath there is the trick stuff—dealer-installed minitraction bars that do a neat job of fending off axle tramp.

often than not, summer is a three-month sentence at an open-hearth furnace. Our test machine had air conditioning and that barely did the job on a 90-degree day, so you couldn't say much for natural ventilation. Some of the difficulty is attributable to the lack of more than two air registers above seat level and a poor central location. The Saab, bless its heart, had its fresh air outlets placed directly in front of the driver and passengers so that the breeze traveled as short a route as possible. Even at 65, you could zip along with almost no wind noise (something our SST could claim only when standing still), and yet enjoy draft-free ventilation. The reason the Swedes came out better is they still take their air supply from a high-pressure area and exhaust it in a low one, behind the rear-quarter window. American's intent is well taken but this is one time when Yankee ingenuity did not triumph. Maybe next year.

One of the reasons why the Javelin looks so good in the first place is that the windshield is raked back to 59 degrees, like the Toronado, Eldorado, and Riviera. It, therefore, enjoys some of the exclusive rub-off as compared to Mustangs and Camaros, which look almost bolt upright at 52 degrees. The ventless, curved side windows don't hurt anything either except the effort, wear, and shade factors. By its very shape, curved side-glass means that, in order for the window to fit properly when closed, the unit must travel

"... around the bend and I'm going again." Javelins are that kind of car. A healthy mix of heavy-duty suspension and Goodyear Wide Treads does a marvelous job. Another point is the quick steering, one of the lowest ratios available in the industry. Trans Am anyone?

inward as well as upward when cranked from an open position. And they do, but as a consequence: a) two men and a boy are needed to go from open to closed because, to seal properly, the glass exerts a good deal of pressure against the rubber (this condition has been partially corrected with a running change in later cars); b) the seal will tend to wear quickly because of this pressure; c) with little support for the large glass, except at full-open or full-closed, the window will loosen in its moorings and rattle (both of ours did at under 3,000 miles); and d) the whole curved side-glass business legislates that the roof is rather narrow and doesn't do a very pleasant job of shading the occupants at any time other than high noon. One redeeming factor is that with a no-vent configuration, you do not get much buffeting effect with the windows down.

But the styling, conveniences, interior space, fresh air ventilation, and the lot of it doesn't amount to a hill of beans if you can't offer performance in several dimensions. You've got to have a performance reputation. On the first spin around the block, we knew this wasn't the latest version of the tepid Kenosha, Wisconsin, Airflight. Five-and-a-half-inch rims shod with E-70 Goodyear Wide Treads got the Javelin about on its heavy-duty suspension, fat antisway bar, and stiff shocks in a most un-American way. Sure, the boys back in dairyland haven't got all the milk-truck-like harshness out of the setup yet, but it's 100 percent improved over what they had last year when we did the Rogue 290. Part of this ride harshness was our fault because we discovered that 30 pounds psi in the tires enabled "Hambone, Hambone, where you been?," "Through the esses, and I'm going again"–type fun and games, and we weren't about to give back the extra air. On a

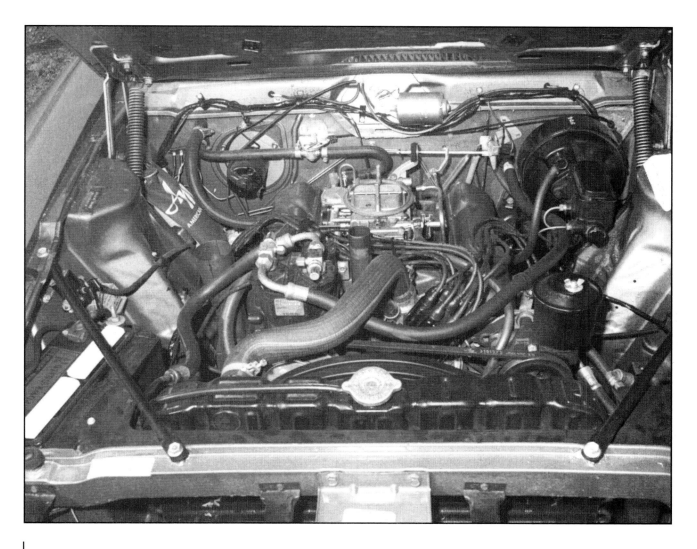

In the engine compartment, the 343 was reliable, started first crack out of the bucket, but it will not make it against the majority of the contenders in the field. The standard carb is a Carter AFB that interchanges with a Holley 1-14 easily.

long series of tight right- and left-hand curves, the quick response, the time it took to go from one steady state to another, was pleasingly impressive. And all this flat tracking despite about 350 more pounds on the front than rear—heavy-duty suspension and Wide Tread tires truly work wonders.

As long as we're kindled with childlike enthusiasm, how about those Bendix power disc/drum brakes? Flying over unfamiliar mountain roads requires a great deal of faith and aircraft arresting hook-like stops in abundance and variety, and Javelin's brakes were all we could want. Best of all, you could feel and even control the point at which tire adhesion gave way.

Even the steering was fast. American Motors was smart here by putting out some special ratios for the Javelin, quicker ratios than you can get almost anywhere else in America. For example, we had a 17.1:1 overall power unit that used 3.6 turns to get the wheel from

1968 JAVELIN SST

PRICE
As tested . . . . $4,122 F.O.B. Detroit

ENGINE
Cylinders 8
Bore and stroke 4.08x3.23
Displacement . . . . .343 ci
Compression ratio . . . . .10.2 to 1
Maximum horsepower . . . . .280 @ 4,800 rpm
Maximum torque . . . . .365 @ 3,000 rpm
Valves:
    Intake . . . . .2.025 in.
    Exhaust . . . . .1.625 in.
Camshaft:
    Lift . . . . .477 in. intake, .477 exhaust
    Duration . . . . .302°
Carburetion . . . . .Carter AFB
Exhaust system . . . . .2.0-in. exhaust pipe,
                                            2.0-in. tailpipe

TRANSMISSION
Type . . . . .Borg-Warner 3-speed auto
                                            with torque convertor
Ratios: 1st 1.47:1
          2nd 2.40:1
          3rd 1.00:1
          4th . . . . .N/A

DIFFERENTIAL
Type . . . ."Twin-Grip" Dana Spicer
Ring gear diameter . . . . .8.75 in.
Ratio 3.54-to-1

BRAKES
Type . . . . .Disc front, drum rear
Dimensions: Front . . . . .11.19 in.
            Rear . . . . .10.00 in.
Swept area . . . . .371 in.

SUSPENSION
Front . . . . .Ind. direct action coils
Rear . . . . .Parallel leaf springs
Stabilizer . . . . .94-in. diameter
Tires .Goodyear E-70 Wide Tread
Rims . . . . .5.5-in. wide
Steering gear:
    Type . . . . .Power-Saginaw
    Ratio 17.1-to-1
    Turning circle . . . . .36.8 ft.
    Turns of steering wheel,
        lock to lock 3.6

PERFORMANCE
Standing quarter-mile . . . . .90 mph in 15.40 sec.

DIMENSIONS
Wheelbase . . . . .109.0 in.
Front track . . . . .58.36 in.
Rear track . . . . .57.0 in.
Overall height . . . . .51.81 in.
Overall width . . . . .71.89 in.
Overall length . . . . .189.22 in.
Curb weight . . . . .3,427 lbs.
Test weight . . . . .3,480 lbs.
Crankcase capacity . . . . .5 qt.
Cooling system . . . . .14 qt.
Fuel tank . . . . .19 gal.

lock-to-lock. The standard ratio is 24.1:1 (5.1 turns), and an optional 19.3:1 (4.0 turns) is the quickest. But, alas, there is a fly in the ointment. On most power-equipped steerings, it is possible to get ahead of the power by intricate low-speed maneuvering. On our Javelin you could do it under certain conditions in regular low-speed maneuvering. Zonk, when pulling away from behind a parked car—no steering—at least until the regulating valve got re-synched.

Acceleration—now there's another rub. In order to cut it in the performance image department, a 343 280-horsepower Javelin with a 3.54 final gear ratio must be prepared to turn a minimum of 15 seconds flat in the quarter-mile or no trophies. You know what the competition is in these classes? 327 Chevelles and Camaros, that's what! And there just isn't any way. Dave Potter, AMC's engine-design ace, revised the port layout of the 343 to increase volumetric efficiency (lower emissions), as well as the intake manifold for better low rpm fuel distribution with quad carburetors. But it isn't enough. The dealer-installed camshaft kit we had in our 290 last time ought to be the plan with the 343 and then another one above that. Just to show you what can happen to the best-laid plans of engine designers, after the boys found a few extra ponies, someone went and put the bottom radiator hose dead on the fuel pump outlet line, thereby insuring nice warm gasoline for a Carter AFB-lean (cleaner air package) to begin with.

On the street, the car felt pretty good, but a 16.41–87.20 at San Fernando showed everyone in the G/Stock class they had nothing to fear. Part of this lackadaisicalness can be laid at a millstone weight of 3,480 pounds. So, off came the Carter and on went a 1-14 Holley we had left over from something or other. By this time we had also discovered the gravity of the radiator hose-to-fuel pump situation. This was fixed by shortening the hose by about two inches and wrapping the line in aluminum foil. In went a fresh set of N-12Y Champion spark plugs and out to the track we went again. Surprise! A full second is gone from the elapsed time and the speed is up to 90.45 miles per hour, still not in Camaro or Firebird range, but close. At least the car is consistent, battling out nearly identical back-to-back runs and manually selecting shifts on the Borg-Warner three-speed automatic. At normal traffic speed, the box exhibits aggravatingly lethargic gear changes, but occasionally when the line pressure comes up at high rpm, the sequence is acceptably positive. Not as good as a TorqueFlite or Turbo Hydra-Matic mind you, but they're getting on.

It is difficult to know whether or not the Javelin will be the most popular car of this season or if it will be another Marlin. If GM or Ford had brought it out, they'd sell like money was going out of style the day after tomorrow. The sad truth is, however, at least some people will refrain from buying the car on the same grounds that they didn't buy a Studebaker in '64 or a Packard in '56. Another fact of life American automobile makers in general are going to have to face more and more is that their products are not wise investments in some cases. One acquaintance commented after seeing the Javelin, "Sure it's a beautiful car, but they'll probably change it completely in two years. I bought a new '65 Mustang for $2,400 and now it's only worth $1,400 on the market. A '65 VW would have been $1,700 and is worth more than my car now. Why have I got to be the sucker?"

If a person looks close enough, this factor may work in favor of American Motors, since what you get for the money here (base price is $109 lower than the Mustang, $89 less than the Camaro and the SST car-for-car, and $350 less than the Cougar) seems more than what is available elsewhere. What Mary Wells ought to do is get all the machines in the personal car segment, flip them over, and have a point-by-point comparison of the pieces. Things like super-big brakes, a porcelainized exhaust system (with galvanized steel wrapped mufflers), and just plain beefy construction has to be worth something. Maybe $4,122.

Be this as it may, the Javelin, at least the one we had, seemed an easy car to live with. As with Nash and AM for almost 30 years now, the car has a unit frame/body structure and is, therefore, more solid than most. Along about January, a new 390-cid engine is slated for introduction and this will almost unquestionably give the machine even wider appeal than we think it will have as is. Another possibility is a Javelin station wagon version and that could be a sensation overnight if handled properly. American Motors is searching for the answer to difficulties of the last few years and if concepts like the Javelin prove successful, you can expect bolder moves to keep the momentum going. Would you believe Mary Wells in a roadster?

CLASS WITH A CAPITAL GTO

ERIC DAHLQUIST
Hot Rod, February 1968

When you're talking about supercars, don't forget the one that started the whole thing — Indian

Click. The world is on. GTO. You can see the letters form on her lips through the panes of laminated safety glass separating the cars as they move side by side up the long grade. In the west, the sun has just plunged behind the brush-carpeted hills, and the sky is a radiant reddish-purple above the topmost crests. But the only light in the pass comes from the valley ahead.

The freeway concrete is smooth except at the expansion joints, which the tires leap two or three times a second, and the taut suspension makes a slight adjustment for it. You are part of a river of light hurtling through a half dark space in the Santa Monica mountains, and there is somebody's neatly-coiffured secretary looking at the flowing shape beside her VW in the fast lane. She cannot know that the dialogue between the UniRoyal Fastrack Red Lines and the road is a Xerox of an XKE, that Herb Alpert is doing a couple of fantastic sets in this recording booth Pontiac calls a multiplex stereo radio, or that the warm pale glow from the instrument panel makes it almost seem you were on the autobahn getting ready to overtake a 250 SL Mercedes, but it doesn't matter. All she knows is that it is one of the most beautiful cars she has ever seen, and it would cause about as much furor in movietown as being carried down Hollywood Boulevard in a sedan chair. Or on Van Nuys Boulevard, on a Wednesday night.

It is only three weeks until Christmas, and the lights from all the strings of colored bulbs lacing the street swirl and reflect in unreal, psychedelic green, yellow, and white streams over the slippery, lacquered hood scoops. A kid slides up to the light in a raked Chevelle SS 396 with unpolished "Americans." He appraised the GTO's C/Gas idle and the lines with a cool, detached eye—an eye that has seen blown/injected 'Vettes on this same boulevard—and notices there are no cheater slicks. The car has Michigan plates, and in Motown they don't run cheater slicks; everything is rolling starts.

"What'll it turn?"

"Ninety-nine at Irwindale."

Last year, Pontiac was an innovator with hideaway winshield wipers; now all GM lines have them. This year, it's the energy-absorbing bumper. Face it—this is Pontiac's era.

From a distance, you could almost swear the GTO was a Firebird. And that's a good thing, but there is room for design improvement.

"What gear?"

"3.90s."

"Pure stock?"

"Yeah."

He looks the car over once more very carefully, absorbing each bulge and line and the hood-mounted tach. The caution light in the cross street blinks on. "Boss," he says, idling away as the signal goes green.

Such are the life and times of the GTO driver. "We wonder," said one Oldsmobile man, "when Pontiac will rejoin General Motors." Pontiac grappled within the same design perimeter as the rest of the divisions, but their A-bodied Tempest stands classically alone. From a distance, you could almost swear it was a Firebird. And that's a good thing because the Firebird is a small car, and any time you can make a bigger car's style as appealing as a small one, you've done it all. Besides this, they've got the "bumper of the year." Pontiac always comes up with something to make everybody else in the industry wonder why they even bother. Last year, it was the hood-mounted tach and recessed wipers. The year before, it was the SOHC six, and the year before that Ram-Air. Way back in 1959, they had mag wheels and bucket seats.

This time, it's the bumper. Remember years ago when fiberglass was the new miracle compound and athletic types were going around with ball peen hammers showing everybody how the stuff would bounce back following impact? Well, now all those ball peens have been traded in for crowbars, and they do it on TV. A full complement of Hollywood extras flogged the front bumper of our test car for the better part of 12 hours in a commercial announcing GTO had been chosen "car of the year" by our sister publication, *Motor Trend*, and all the pounding didn't faze the car's nose a bit. The voice of Pontiac, actor Paul Richards, even took a few whacks at it when he wasn't telling the world why the GTO was the great one, and if you don't believe cool Paul Richards, you don't believe anybody.

The bumper presents quite a case. It is energy-absorbing, so the safety people love it, and at least half your parallel parking difficulties are solved. Another aspect is that the thing is molded and therefore can be quite easily cast into any shape the designer's imagination might unfold. Then there is the bumper's paint. Nobody has said much about it, but it doesn't seem to chip or peel and, in fact, actually flexes with the bumper. Perhaps super-paint will be the hot item from "Indianland" in '69.

Inside, there is the instrument panel of the year. Nearly every other American manufacturer sees the dash as a place where gadgeteers can run rampant in the worst traditions of our pure vinyl society. Nobody seems to realize that the dashboard is like your wife: it stares back at you every morning. You don't need a chrome raspberry to remind you that you laid out four grand for the car. Besides that, it's handy to know your oil pressure's gone because you just picked up a punji spike in the pan or that you could have saved the radiator from boiling over in heavy traffic by circulating the water faster if only you had known that the engine was heating up in the first place.

Getting into a GTO is like putting on a good suit—it feels right. "Fits me just fine," said Can-Am driver Chuck Parsons when he tried the car out, relaxed in the beautiful bucket seats and tried a practice throw from second to third—a distance spanned instantly by the Hurst shifter. And the seats are for sitting in—not put-ons with little function, but relax-into types, get-comfortable-in loungers for a drive to 'Vegas or 'Frisco with lots of lateral support. And who cares if it isn't real leather? It looks almost as good, the interior all in black from head to toe and enough flat pliable window crank knobs and padding to make budding Naderites shout hosanna, but not enough to destroy the car's appearance.

This GTO is painted the brightest, smoothest red known to man—red outside, black inside. We wouldn't have it any other way. We know the car has been carefully prepared by Pontiac for several road tests and a commercial, so the lacquer is rubbed out like a vermilion mirror and the panels fit very well . . . and representatives of other Detroit manufacturers warn us how this is a bogus machine and isn't anything like what the dealers sell the kiddies. Carpers and criers of Motown, you lose. When was the last time you saw one of those '64 or '65 Tigers falling to pieces in the street? Besides, what's wrong with making the car the way it was designed to be in the first place? If it shows up the work of the UAW and the dealer's new-car prep, all the better. Why should American automotive consumers always aim for mediocrity?

But there is room for some design improvement. In the front fenders and doors, there is that hollow tin-Indian echo. Maybe it's the way the panels are laid out, or the compound curves, or the inner braces, but the Buick GS 400 seemed a lot more solid, especially in the bow section. Or how about a little less vibration in the steering wheel, Mr. DeLorean? Or some deadener in the trunk to kill the resonance from the best-sounding mufflers in America, a din that can drive you nuts at low speed and under load. That's the thing about having a near-perfect car—a little flaw looks like Mount Everest.

Now you've got to admit that's a pretty fine profile. GTOs have always had that coiled, ready-to-spring quality about them—maybe that's why they're called tigers. They don't lack for a lot, but there are a few flaws. Like the headroom isn't the all-time greatest, there's too much road shock in the steering but not enough feel, and some of the sheet metal isn't the stoutest. They don't give this car away, and things like 343 bucks for the Ram-Air induction package keep people on welfare from getting too interested. But it does work, and a century mark performance probably will improve after first of the year, when the new heads and cams are due.

One thing that's been a thorn in the side of Pontiac since the whole supercar business got started in 1964 is that the 442 Olds always had a measurable edge on handling. You all know from last month about the new 112-inch wheelbase configuration and what it has done to banish freeway hop, but it also has enabled Pontiac to close the maneuverability gap a bit with the "bad guys" in Lansing. In fact, it is not an overstatement that the '68 GTO is probably the best-balanced car they ever built.

Surprisingly, too, were the G77x14 UniRoyal "Fastraks" that *may* just be the stickiest of the new breed of maximum performance tires. Back in the old days of 1964, when the original red-line came out for the then-new GTO, it seemed that the manufacturer believed his own ad copy more than the performance capabilities of the tire. Funny thing was that the rest of the industry, especially Firestone, with the help of a couple of thousand kids who couldn't wait and put Indy skins on their mags, brought out "wide-oval" designs of one kind or other and left Royal at the gate—literally. But things may have changed. Hard as it may seem, the GTO ran only one and a half to two tenths of a second slower than with a set of slicks.

So enough, you say, how did the car run? That is what the GTO is all about, isn't it? Right, and even hedged with the new anti-air pollution calibrations, the thing made 97 miles per hour in 14.70 seconds the first time we had it out. New AC 44S plugs, removal of the power steering belt, an unplugged alternator (so it wouldn't charge), and a high of 99.11–14.48 in strictly pure stock form came up. Adding a set of Bill Casler's 7-inch-wide, 26-inch-diameter cheaters dropped the elapsed time to 14.32. One reason why the slicks made a minimal gain was that they just plain had too much bite, bogging the engine on all but the "to-the-wood-sidestep-the-clutch" starts.

Our strip session happened to be out at Irwindale Raceway during the week, so we were able to make almost all runs—back-to-back—eight straight, a break, and eight more straight. Know what? The car wasn't affected much by continual hard abuse. In fact, the temperature gauge never got past normal. In 16 straight passes (64 shifts, plus "flogging" another car as well), we missed one gear change and that was it. And behind every good run there had better be a good stop or it's into the "tules" for a little instant off-road action. Don't sweat it; the GTOs brakes are right there: disc front, drum rear. It stops like A. J. Foyt at Riverside running into quicksand.

What it all means, pal, is that Pontiac has built one heck of a consistent, competitive racer. Chrysler Corporation, especially, wonders how a machine that has fresh air induction,

1968 PONTIAC GTO

PRICE
As tested $4,315.45

ENGINE
Cylinders 8
Bore and stroke 4.122x3.754
Displacement .... 400 ci
Compression ratio .... 10.75 to 1
Maximum horsepower .... 350 @ 5,000 rpm
Maximum torque .... 445 @ 3,000 rpm
Valves:
   Intake .... 1.917 in.
   Exhaust .... 1.603 in.
Camshaft:
   Lift .... .438 intake, .438 exhaust
   Duration .... 244°
Carburetion 1 4-barrel
Exhaust system .... 2.25-in. exhaust pipe,
                           2.00-in. tailpipe

TRANSMISSION
Type .... 4-speed standard
Ratios: 1st 2:52:1
        2nd 1.88:1
        3rd 1.46:1
        4th 1.00:1

DIFFERENTIAL
Type .... Limited slip
Ring gear diameter .... 8.125 in.
Ratio .... 3.90 to 1

BRAKES
Type .... Disc, front; drum, rear
Dimensions: Front .... 11.12 in.
            Rear .... 9.85 in.
Swept area .... 323.6 in.

SUSPENSION
Front .... Independent, coil
Rear .... Link coil
Stabilizer .... 1.00-in. diameter
Tires G77x14
Rims .... 6-in. wide
Steering gear:
   Type .... Saginaw power
   Ratio .... 22 to 1
   Turning circle .... 40.9 ft.
   Turns of steering wheel,
     lock to lock 4.2

PERFORMANCE
0-30 .... 3.0 sec.
0-40 .... 3.4 sec.
0-50 .... 5.0 sec.
0-60 .... 5.9 sec.
Standing quarter-mile .... 106.64 mph in 13.56 sec.

DIMENSIONS
Wheelbase .... 108 in.
Front track .... 58.0 in.
Rear track .... 58.0 in.
Overall height .... 51.6 in.
Overall width .... 70.9 in.
Overall length .... 183.6 in.
Curb weight .... N/A
Test weight 3,240
Crankcase capacity .... 5 qt.
Cooling system .... N/A
Fuel tank .... 17 gal.

a different cam, and valve train gets by in NHRA classing with a horsepower rating identical to a car that doesn't; but don't worry about such trivialities. It's to your advantage, isn't it? At 3,800 pounds, the machine is no featherweight, so you need all the breaks you can get.

So there we were a few days later—Managing Editor Don Evans at the wheel, his son Mike, and I—driving home from the Rams/Packers game (a game the Rams won 27-24 in the last 30 seconds) into a fantastically beautiful palm-studded California sunset. This was Don's first experience with the car, and he was impressed—not so much by the attention it drew from the old and young alike, but from the lithe, limber way it threaded through traffic. After a long while, he turned and said, "How sweet it is." Indeed, my friend, how sweet.

THE JET SET

ERIC DAHLQUIST
Hot Rod, March 1968

In one fell swoop, Ford has answered all your cards and letters.
The carmaker's answer is called the Mustang Cobra Jet

Everybody in Detroit is mad at us—except Ford. With the help of about 2,000 of you in readerland, who dutifully filled out the November issue ballots and mailed it to Dearborn, ("Ford's Ultimate Supercars," November 1967 HRM) several key executives who doubted that Ford cars lacked competitive street performance reversed their opinion (under a write-in confrontation with the buyer) and—presto—a new marketing direction was embarked upon. This was not the greatest news to the rest of Motown's supercar purveyors who were happily slicing up a big, trend-setting market while the Total Performance people suffered. Ford's lacking competitive street performance was a standard cocktail-hour joke, and we went and ruined the whole deal. The laughing stopped when the first 428 Cobra Jet "instant eliminator" rolled into the sunlight. The Cobra Jet will be the utter delight of every Ford lover and the bane of all the rest because, quite frankly, it is probably the fastest regular production sedan ever built.

We are tempted to accept the credit for the Cobra Jet's existence, but the talented, young, excited engineers in Ford's special vehicles department (and Bob Tasca) deserve the bows. Our function was to editorially point out an existing deficiency that any kid on Woodward Avenue could have told them. Ford has had good pieces all along, but getting them into a package was the problem.

Our package was a little late in getting here. First it was the strike, then it was the bad weather, and one thing or another—even this issue's regular deadline—came and went without a Cobra Jet in sight. These 11th-hour deals normally turn people off, yet the Mustang we picked up at Holman-Moody-Stroppe was worth the inconvenience. The frustration disappeared the first time we let it happen—"waaah"—the secondaries came open and you realized most races would end in low gear. The would-be competitor cannot believe his eyes. No Mustang, outside of Tasca's "Mystery 7," has ever moved this quickly.

Of course our car was not quite representative. By special order, the sound-deadening material was omitted, so this Mustang was a light 3,240 pounds. As a result, it was quite

Yes, "Virginia," the Ford supercar program is alive and living on the streets. Advance billing forecast is 13.30, 106 miles-per-hour performance. Nonpower-assisted steering and sticky tires allow for rapidly accelerated bicep development.

noisy inside—perhaps in the same decibel range as the Mark IV GT that Gurney and Foyt raced in against Le Mans and won. Motoring through the countryside in a 50-gallon steel echo chamber can have a tiring effect in doses of 300 miles, but we got used to it. We also adapted to the high-effort steering that a nose-heavy car like this has without power (it's a drag car, right?), and in the long run everybody ought to have biceps like Steve Reeves.

Out on the freeway, the Jet churns through traffic like a broken-field runner, but the transition from one steady state to another (response)—as in lane changing—took longer than it should. On moderately rough roads, the car's poor ride showed up immediately, which is a factor of the heavy-duty suspension package with high-rate springs. On very tight downhill curves, there was noticeable understeer, similar to the 390-powered Mustang machine we had a year ago. A very light rear can get the whole thing drifting sideways at unique angles quite easily. That's always been the hangup with a heavy engine like the 428 in a small car like a Mustang, and it's a real challenge to get the machine to handle as well as this one does.

Whatever time is lost on turns, however, is immediately regained on the straightaway. The thing that makes this engine run is the pieces we saw last summer at Tasca Ford in East Providence, Rhode Island, and at Bill Holbrook's portion of the Experimental Garage in Dearborn. And, the 2.06-inch-diameter intake valves and 1.625-inch exhausts in the old '63 heads are the biggest factors and are items Ford has needed on the street for years. They even added a quickie (and cheapie) cold-air package that consists of a lay-on rubber-ringed steel insert designed to seal the top of the air filter to the hood. Tasca's unit, though probably more costly, looked better and was more effective since it picked up air directly from the grille and in a high-pressure area. The center of the hood is not the ultimate spot to catch the wind. An alternate plan would have been a

Actually, the Cobra Jet deal is an optional package on several lines of Ford cars. These are subdivided into high-performance and normal versions. Consequently there are two of everything, except the basic block. Pistons come with 10.75:1 and 11.50:1 ratios. There are hydraulic and mechanical tappet cams, regular and deep-sump oil pans, 735 and 785 cfm Holley carbs, and more.

NASCAR-type arrangement through the plenum chamber like the Z-28 Camaro, Buick Gran Sport, or pilot Cobra Jet that was comprised mostly of an existing Holman-Moody unit.

Not that the car really needs it, mind you, for it's already bred well into the state of overkill. First pass in the car at Irwindale was a 13.90-103.96 with street tires and super wheel hop. Clamping the spring leaves and removing the accessory belts put us at 13.56-106.64—the fastest-running Pure Stock in the history of man. Ford did not foul up in the rating game footwork, either, slapping on an innocent 335 horsepower, and NHRA bought it lock, stock, and barrel—sliding the Cobra Jet into C/S, C/SA or, with bigger tires, SS/E. For once, anyone can be competitive in a drag class and with hardly an adjustment. Think of it, if you act fast and get one before a lot of them are floating around, you can go to the local strip and single-handedly make a complete shambles out of the class and the eliminator.

It didn't start out that way, but since we had just finished with a Firebird Ram-Air 400, a comparison between it and the Cobra Jet Mustang was inevitable. On ultimate, brute, mind-bending acceleration, the Cobra Jet won hands down. But do not lose the fact that it has 28 more inches and 260 pounds less weight than a very nimble Firebird. Both machines were equipped with heavy-duty suspension, yet the Pontiac's ride was far less harsh, produced measurably better handling and excellent low-speed maneuverability. Even without sound deadeners and the normal new car prep, the Mustang seemed to be a more solid platform, and it says a lot for Ford quality control, although the Pontiac's finish could not be faulted.

You get into the tacky area when you start talking price. The sticker total for the Cobra Jet Mustang was $3,643 or almost a grand more than a base 2-plus-2 Mustang fastback. Pontiac wanted $3,807 for the Firebird, but it had custom wheels, an adjustable steering wheel, a deluxe interior, plus an AM/FM radio. Ford officials were quick to point out that our particular Cobra Jet was one of the first batch intended exclusively for drag strip work.

"What you have is our low-line stripped Mustang with a Cobra Jet package. You can order the package on any Fairlane, Montego (modern French for the now passé Comet), Cougar, or Mustang and get the luxury options you want." But that's just the point. If a low-level Mustang brings $3,643, how dear would one be that was equipped to the level of the Firebird?

Another thing is the service gap. The way the 428 is jammed into the engine compartment makes only brave souls with asbestos skin attempt the time-honored ritual of replacing the spark plugs. This dreary aspect is reflected in a mechanic's standard flat rate of $30 for the job. Admittedly, the street flogger doesn't do as much work on his car as a decade ago, but easily accessible plugs are basic requirements. That's one of the things that "did in" the street hemi's popularity.

Such is Ford's great leap forward—the Cobra Jet. The mere fact these Dearborn rocket sleds are coming off the production line deserves some kind of award. However, it is no cause for complacency, since competitors like Pontiac and Chevy are not far behind, if at all, and will surely meet this potential threat with further escalations of their own. A last fine point for consideration is that Ford's nonsupercars such as its Country Squire wagons, are in need of a little sauce, too. They're reliable as a stone chisel but fall prey to beetles off the mark, and even on the way to the movies this doesn't show "mama" much class.

Fortunately for Ford, their supporters from the good old days are still legion, and if they weren't, the strength of a single Cobra Jet blast-off will put thousands into orbit for the nearest auto loan department. Demonstrating its new confidence in the whole project, Ford has scheduled a trial balloon of 5,000 units (or about half the demand). It's so very close to what Ford has needed all these years that it can't miss. Funny, only a few people realized it.

MUSTANG COBRA JET

PRICE
As tested $3,643.40

ENGINE
Cylinders 8
Bore and stroke 4.13x3.98
Displacement . . . . .428 ci
Compression ratio .10.6 to 1
Maximum horsepower . . . . .335 @ 5,400 rpm
Maximum torque . . . . .440 @ 3,400 rpm
Valves:
    Intake . . . . .2.06 in.
    Exhaust . . . . .1.625 in.
Camshaft:
    Lift .481 intake, .490 exhaust
    Duration . . . . .290°
Carburetion . . . . .Single four-barrel Holley
Exhaust system . . . . .N/A.

TRANSMISSION
Type 4-speed
Ratios: 1st 2.32
         2nd 1.69
         3rd 1.29
         4th 1.00

DIFFERENTIAL
Type . . . . .Nodular 31-spline
Ring gear diameter . . . . .9 in.
Ratio . . . . .3.89 to 1

BRAKES
Type .Disc front, drum rear
Dimensions: Front . . . . .11.38 in.
              Rear . . . . .10.00 in.
Swept area . . . . .330 in.

SUSPENSION
Front . . . . .Independent, drag strut
Rear . . . . .Leaf spring
Stabilizer . . . . .84 in. diameter
Tires F-70x14
Rims . . . . .6-in. wide
Steering gear:
    Type . . . . .Manual
    Ratio . . . . .16 to 1

PERFORMANCE
0-30 . . . . .3.0 sec.
0-40 . . . . .3.4 sec.
0-50 . . . . .5.0 sec.
0-60 . . . . .5.9 sec.
Standing quarter-mile . . . . .106.64 mph in 13.56 sec.

DIMENSIONS
Wheelbase . . . . .108 in.
Front track . . . . .58.0 in.
Rear track . . . . .58.0 in.
Overall height . . . . .51.6 in.
Overall width . . . . .70.9 in.
Overall length . . . . .183.6 in.
Curb weight . . . . .N/A
Test weight 3240
Crankcase capacity .5 qt.
Cooling system . . . . .N/A
Fuel tank . . . . .17 gal.

HERE COME DE JUDGE

STEVE KELLY
Hot Rod, December 1968

Not to be outdone, Pontiac joins the "economy" supercar battle with a machine right out of GTO territory

Nearly every automaker tuned into performance cars has introduced their own version of an "economy" supercar in the past year. Some have bold identifications; others merely carry a low price sticker. While the economy bit has been good for enthusiasts and manufacturers alike, there's more to it than low price, from the factory's standpoint. This is the only method open for most to grab a larger share of the supercar market. Prior to this, they'd found little success in bucking head-on with the super leader, Pontiac's GTO. The GTO has led the field in sales and prestige since its introduction in '64. And if that's not enough to discourage even the best product planner among Pontiac's competition, here they are in '69 with their own idea of an economy supercar. It's a new game, fellas, with a fresh player on the field.

We first met the Judge at Ubly Dragway, a pleasant spot about 100 miles north of Detroit in the Saginaw Bay area. Besides its charm, Ubly is remote from inquisitive eyes, and since we tested the Judge prior to introduction, this helped. Along with the other first few thousand off the line, this one finished in an eye-catching Dayglo red. From the front, we could tell very little difference between the Judge and a standard GTO except for the fact that the headlights were exposed, but this is often part of a GTO. The difference was scant. But from the backside, there's no mistaking it. A full-width rear deck spoiler is a standard item, and it's as different from current air-spoiler designs as this car — or the regular GTO — is from its marketplace rivals. The 60-inch-wide panel is horizontally placed and is supported by a pair of stands on the deck lid. The spoiler's leading edge is 3.5 inches off the trunk surface. Its full-width design better be noticed by anyone resting their hand on the fender edge while the deck is lowered; otherwise a lesson in how compressible human skin is might quickly be learned.

At first sight, we considered the spoiler a bit ostentatious. We changed our opinion soon afterward, though. Like anything unusual, it takes getting used to. Drag racers will quickly realize a benefit from the fiberglass spoiler, as its rear placement on the car adds

So here it is, Pontiac's method of putting the competition in deep thought.

weight to the tail end, desirable for weight transfer on acceleration. If the car catches on as well as we think it will, Pontiac dealers better stock these spoilers. They'll fit in with all '68 and '69 GTOs and Tempests and could turn out to be the next best thing to an additive decal for street machine status.

Performance was a bit less on this GTO-derived car than we've experienced on previous GTO tests. But we were far from disappointed with the results. Anytime a supercar in ultra-stock forms even breaks into the 14-second region, we're happy. And this car did more than break into it; it was never out. Our best quarter-mile clocking was a 14.41-second elapsed time and top speed at 99.55 miles per hour. With two good-sized riders (driver and passenger) aboard, we pulled a 14.83 elapsed time and 97.50 miles per hour top end. It would probably take a full complement of passengers to slow the Judge down to where most super-machines run normally.

We didn't equal many previous tests because this car was kept as absolutely "showroom." It's a matter of habit for quickening a car's times to increase front tire pressure, experiment with rear air settings, remove the air-cleaner element, advance timing slightly, remove accessory drive belts, and loosen the alternator belt. None of these were attempted during our test. Not that we didn't have time, but this was based more on testing how well a really street-comfort machine would work than to find the car's absolute capabilities. We're very familiar with a 400-ci Pontiac's potential. This was the first time we'd restricted ourselves to direct off-the-street-and-onto-the-strip performance. The experience was entirely our pleasure. Without reservation, we'd project mid-to-high-12-second clockings on a properly prepared Judge.

Worth noting in regard to our test is that this particular car had power steering, front disc brakes with power assistance, electric windows, and a couple of other weight-adding, performance-robbing extras.

It might seem—from the foregoing text—that the Judge is a stranger to the GTO. That's hardly the situation. The Judge carries GTO nameplates and is, in essence, a little brother to the widely fabled "Tiger" from Wide-Track Boulevard. It fits into the "economy" classification. A bench seat instead of buckets is standard, trim rings aren't included on the standard

Sure it goes, but supercars should stop well, too. This one does. We registered successive straight-line stops from 80 and 60 miles per hour without brake fade and virtually no lockup on the disc-braked Judge. We asked Pontiac reps a lot of questions before concluding the hardtop coupe is a big sales threat to its competitors. Bet it gives older brother GTO a good run as well. The rear spoiler is Judge's most distinctive item, but there are others—like Ram-Air, rally wheels, bright colors, and groovy trim. The proposed price and performance brand this one a winner for '69.

1969 PONTIAC GTO/JUDGE

PRICE
As tested ....N/A

ENGINE
Type ....OHV V-8
Cylinders 8
Bore & Stroke 4.12x3.75
Displacement 400
Compression ratio 10.75:1
Horsepower ....366 @ 5,100 rpm
Torque ....445 lbs.-ft. @ 3,600 rpm
Valves:
  Intake ....2.11-in. dia.
  Exhaust ....1.77-in. dia.
Camshaft:
  Lift ....414 in. intake, .413 in. exhaust
  Duration ....288° intake, 302° exhaust
Lifters ....Hydraulic
Carburetion ....1 4-barrel Quadrajet
Exhaust system ....Dual w/low restriction muffler

TRANSMISSION
Type ....Close ratio 4-speed w/Hurst shifter
Ratios: 1st 2.20:1
        2nd 1.64:1
        3rd 1.28:1
        4th 1.00:1

DIFFERENTIAL
Type ....Limited slip
Ring gear diameter ....8.125 in.
Ratio 3.90:1

BRAKES
Type ....Front disc/rear drum
Dimensions: Front disc ....11.1 in.
            Rear drum ....9.5 in.
Swept area: Front ....323.6 sq. in.
            Rear ....269.2 sq. in.

SUSPENSION
Front ....Heavy-duty coil
Rear ....Heavy-duty coil
Stabilizer ....1.00-in. diam.
Tires G78-14
Rims ....6-in. wide
Steering:
  Type ....Saginaw Power
  Gear ratio 17.5:1
  Turning circle ....40.9 ft.
  Turn of steering wheel lock to lock 4.2

PERFORMANCE
Standing start quarter-mile
  (best) ....14.41 sec., 99.55 mph
Stopping distances:
  From 80 mph ....261 ft.
  From 60 mph ....159 ft.

DIMENSIONS
Wheelbase ....112 in.
Front track ....60 in.
Rear track ....60 in.
Overall height ....52.3 in.
Overall width ....75.8 in.
Overall length ....201.5 in.
Shipping weight ....3513 lb.
Test weight (pre-production car) ....N/A
Crankcase capacity ....5 qt.
Cooling system ....17.8 qt.
Fuel tank ....21.5 gal.

Rally wheels, and special instrumentation—a strong point on regular GTOs—isn't standard with the Judge.

But on the other hand, there are a couple of exclusives on the "lightweight" that set it off from "big brother," as well as its competition. There's the rear deck spoiler for one; the 400-ci Ram-Air engine; the far-from-overdone side paint trim; the standard 360-horsepower is the best of all. This is the first engine option for GTOs. During our test, we buzzed the engine to 6,000 rpm for shifts, although once we got beyond that point without hurting anything but our elapsed time. There's no reason to go beyond six grand, since maximum horsepower on the Ram-Air engine is developed just past 5,000 rpm. This engine being included with the base car is worth a couple hundred bucks by itself.

Other standard pieces on the Judge are a three-speed all-synchro floor-shifted transmission, complete with Hurst shifter and "T" handle, carpeted flooring, vinyl upholstery, and wood-trimmed dash, à la the GTO.

The car we tested carried a four-speed, with Hurst equipment of course. We recommend either this gearbox or the three-speed Turbo Hydra-Matic over the regular three-speed unit. Not that the 3-speed is bad; it's just that there's a lot more enjoyment, flexibility, and performance to be had from either of the optional transmissions.

Another cute feature on the Ram-Air engine, not exclusive to the Judge, is a dash-controlled, cable-operated flapper valve to shut off the twin hood scoop openings in poor weather. Kinda neat in snow country.

So here it is, Pontiac's method of putting the competition in deep thought. The GTO just wasn't enough; they had to "one-up" the troops in the economy bracket. As in all cars, a few design points could be squared away for the benefit of all concerned. But not many. And a few of them can be cured with a little time and a portion of corporate money. Then customer reaction also plays a big part in planning for the future. We have no idea how long "economy" (a somewhat misleading term if it conjures up thoughts of compact car pricing) performance cars will be in. No matter how long they may stay high in buyer appeal, it won't take much time for the Judge to reach top rating. And if they do fade from popularity, this one'll be there till the very last. So start lining 'em up, cause … "Here come de Judge."

An ad for the GTO Judge.

SHOWROOM RACER

STEVE KELLY
Hot Rod, February 1969

You don't have to wear a driving suit, crash helmet, or goggles in this Dodge à la NASCAR stocker—but if it makes you feel better, go ahead

It's doubtful that I'd ever want a hemi-engined Dodge Charger 500 for my street machine, but if I did, it would be an assembly-line copy of the car used in 17.4 NASCAR action. If it was a tunnel-port 427 Torino that interested me, I'd still be searching for one. You've got to hand it to the Chrysler guys; if they race it, they also sell it. That really doesn't make them heroes, but it does help promote the image of stock car racing. When you can buy your race car, or at least the basics of one, through a dealership, you're a lot closer to racing *real* stock cars.

Charger 500s are specially outfitted models of Charger R/Ts. The differences lie in the same body revisions that contribute to better aerodynamics, primarily to give the stock car racers a better break. This is a limited-edition car right now, since 500 or so must be built in order to comply with the FIA description of "stock." But if they catch on with the buying public, that's fine and more will be built.

The grille, normally inset, is moved forward, flush with the leading edge of the frontal sheet metal. This eliminates the air trap of regular Chargers. In back, the rear window is angled sharply and set in new metal stretched between the sailfins. Standard production Chargers have a near-vertical rear glass, set almost even with the rear seat back. With the 500 configuration, there's a lot more room for a package tray but almost none for a deck lid. There is one, but it's about as big as a glovebox door. As much grain as you'd care to pour into the trunk can be carried, but suitcase size is restricted to ultra-slim designs. With a little jockeying, though, you can fit a lot in there but nonetheless it's not an easy job. Okay, it may be a gripe, but Buddy Baker, Charlie Glotzbach, or Bobby Isaac will probably never care about it or how handy the map pockets align in the doors. They travel light and always on the same road.

In essence, that is what this car is designed to do. It just happens that you can also buy it. Part of the reason is that although Chrysler Divisions may be making money, they're not exactly floating in the green stuff. If they can sell a few of their race car-type

We were a bit early (two months) for the Riverside Motor Trend 500, but it worked out better that way. The good-handling street runner can use help before serious racing.

machines, it helps cover design costs. In most instances, Chrysler has had to work the reverse by facing facsimiles of production cars. Now they've followed the competition by building special edition hardware and furthered this by putting them up for retail purchase. We'll find out later how this marketing philosophy works.

Charger 500 power is by either a 440-ci "wedge" developing 375 horsepower or by the optional 425-horsepower, dual–four-carbureted hemi. In both instances, the transmission choice is between a four-speed manual and a TorqueFlite three-speed automatic. Rear gearing is a 3.23:1, standard for the automatic, and 3.54:1, standard with four-speed. Lower ratios (higher numbers) can be found through dealers' parts counters and are necessary for anything but street operation. Let's face it. If you've got a hemi in *anything*, it's going to be for more than street use.

Each 500 in use for this test was hemi-equipped. Three of 'em were readied for us, but we used only two. One of them, the first four-speed car, was "borrowed" by a person who has not yet been convicted and most of the parts liberated. Due to this unexpected car loan, that's not what the police termed it, we spent most of our time with the automatic car. Given the choice, that's the way I'd have it anyway. Four-speeds are nice and generally a little quicker, but the TorqueFlite is the way to go on the street, and it's certainly no slouch on the track, unless the track has bends in it. Then there's no way an automatic will work there.

Driving ranged from in-town, bumper-to-bumper conditions to high-speed (well, not real high) runs across the desert. We covered a good bit of the southwest, including Riverside International Raceway and Orange County International Raceway. This is the kind

The dash's gauges are well-placed, easy to view, and angled toward the driver. Excellent interior comfort and room is part of the bargain.

of car you make excuses to drive. Other than its altered roof and grille, it is a Charger and everything here applies to "production" Chargers, too.

Equipped as it was, the automatic car is easily one of the best high-speed stockers we've sampled, and quite a few of them have been put in our hands, too. We get irritated at cars that are too quiet and that sometimes diminish handling for the sake of comfort. But noisy cars that handle well will give you an earache within an hour. Handling without earaches is an apt summation of the Charger. The wind glides around this car so smoothly it hardly makes a sound. Keeping a vent window open at 70 miles per hour or thereabouts is rough, but it proves that a good amount of wind directed alongside the car assists with stability.

Steering and braking are good at all speeds. Both cars had power steering and power-assisted front disc brakes, all of which are optional. Low-speed maneuvers produced predictable wheel directing, though washout, or front-tire roll-under, is easy to get if you push the car hard 'round a tight bend. On top end, there's no absence of road feel. Earlier Mopar power steering tended to relieve the driver of contact with the front wheels, but that's all been remedied. Standard brakes are drum-type and of fairly good size for hemi cars, but we wouldn't have one without front discs for street driving; that's a lot of weight out in front. Discs are mandatory. They worked repeatedly in 100-plus miles per hour to zero stops, without complaint or loss of stopping power.

Interior dimensions satisfy the requirements of a six-footer, and that's getting harder to accomplish on intermediate-size cars each year. Rear legroom and headroom is generous, and this is one of the few cars we've tested lately with more seat adjustment than we could use. A neat item for the '69 Dodge is a manual bucket-seat adjuster, which costs just under $40 and allows both vertical and tilt adjustment. There're six variations of it, plus the 10 positions of the regular fore-and-aft adjuster. Since Chargers aren't available with tilting wheels, this item makes comfortable seating possible for drivers of all sizes.

Beginning this year, stock car racing under FIA sanction prohibits use of more than one carburetor, which means Chrysler will be dragging out all its old nonstock, single-four intake manifolds for hemis. They've been using these ever since a ruling forced the removal of the stock dual-four intake and replacing it with the singles. Sometimes it doesn't pay to be too fast. However, drag racers will make out okay, since the 2/4 are still stock and therefore legal.

But it takes more than a pair of four-throat Carters to make a hemi work right. Getting one in the 13s for a quarter-mile in stock clothing is about all one can ask for. Well, we got

The body shape is a real wind-cheater. Air-traps have been designed out. And wait 'til a 500 gets on a superspeedway: half a foot lower and half a light year faster.

it that far, but we had to revert to open headers in order to do so. An open-header 426 ought to catch high 12s, but this was the 3.23-geared automatic, with street plugs (N-10Y Champions), no carb rejetting, ignition at 12 degrees before top dead center on the crank, and total advance not cutting in until past 3,000. With an automatic having a sub-2,000-rpm stall speed, this is like running with one flat tire. The mere fact that it bested 100 miles per hour in this form calls for a Purple Heart. A top elapsed time of 13.80 seconds and a speed of 105.01 miles per hour was the result of this mediocre effort.

We got down to cases with the four-speed. Norm Thatcher put in time here, slipping in a 4.10:1 limited-slip rear gear set and recalibrating the distributor to 49 degrees total, all of

PRICE
Base ....(440 engine, std.) $3591.00 As Tested
$5,261.00
(Hemi: $648.20, extra)

ENGINE
Type ....OHV V-8
Cylinders 8
Bore and stroke ....4.25x3.75 in.
Displacement ....426 ci
Compression ratio 10.25:1
Horsepower ....425 @ 5,000 rpm
Torque ....490 lbs. ft. @ 4,000 rpm
Valves:
   Intake ....2.25-in. dia.
   Exhaust ....1.94-in. dia.
Camshaft:
   Lift ....490-in. intake; .480-in. exhaust
   Duration ....284° intake and exhaust
Tappets ....Mechanical, .028 lash
Carburetion ....Dual Carter AFB
series 4-barrel
Exhaust ....Dual, low restriction

TRANSMISSION
Type ....Manual: floor-mounted shift,
synchro all forward gears
Auto: torque converter with
automatically operated planetary
gear transmission

Ratios:	Automatic	4-speed
1st	2.45:1	2.65:1
2nd	1.45:1	1.93:1
3rd	1.00:1	1.39:1
4th		1.00:1

Clutch ....11-inch diameter, dry-plate
Borg and Beck. 2523-lb. total
spring load

DIFFERENTIAL
Type ....Separable type unit,
friction-bias limited slip with
8.75-in.-dia. ring gear on
automatic. Unitized housing
and 9.75-in.-dia ring
gear, 4-speed
Final drive ratio ....3.23:1, TorqueFlite
4.10:1, 4-speed

BRAKES
Type ....Front disc/rear drum with
power assist. Floating-caliper design
Dimensions:
   Front ....Disc, 11.04-in. dia.
   Rear ....Drum, 10-in. dia.
Total effective area ....131.6 sq. in.
Percent brake effectiveness,
   front 60%

SUSPENSION
Front ....Independent, lateral,
nonparallel control arms
with torsion bars
Rear ....Parallel, 58 in.x2.5 in.,
longitudinal semi-elliptic
rear springs. One piece-type
axle housing
Shocks ....Tubular, double-acting,
1.0-in. piston dia.
Stabilizer ....Front only, .094-in.-dia.
Tires ....F70x15, 4-ply rated, belted
Wheel rim width ....6.0 in.
Steering:
   Type ....Chrysler. recirculating ball
with integral power assist
   Gear ratio 15.7:1
   Overall ratio 18.8:1
   Turning circle ....40.9 ft., curb to curb
   Wheel diameter ....16.0 in.
   Turns lock to lock 3.5

PERFORMANCE
Standing start quarter-mile
   (Automatic): ....13.80 sec., 105.01 mph
   (4-speed): ....13.48 sec., 109.00 mph

FUEL CONSUMPTION
(TorqueFlite-equipped car only)
Best reading ....14.51 mpg
Poorest ....7.3 mpg
Average ....11.05 mpg
Recommended fuel ....Premium

DIMENSIONS
Wheelbase ....117.0 in.
Front track ....59.5 in.
Rear track ....58.5 in.
Overall height ....54.2 in.
Overall width ....76.7 in.
Overall length ....206.6 in.
Shipping weight ....3,305 lbs.
Test weight ....3,740 lbs.
Body/frame construction ....Unit
Fuel tank capacity ....19 gal.

which were at work by 2,500 rpm. In short, it was prepared for a quarter-mile. Orange County International Raceway management consented to let us burn off some more tire rubber, and we did a good job of it.

With the automatic car, we moved the lever as the tach needle passed 5,500 rpm. Stock TorqueFlites have a slight delay, so the actual shift took place at 5,700-5,800 rpm. We buzzed the stick car to six grand for each shift. The 4.10 gear brought us through the traps in high gear at 5,200 rpm, using a 29-inch-diameter tire. A lower gear would certainly help, but the 4.10 is just about the steepest you can use and still get decent street operation. Best time with the stick-shift machine was 13.48 and 109 miles per hour. As we said, a hemi will go in the 12s with external touching-up, but a really good teardown—and money—will put a hemi-stocker at the 11-second break-even mark.

A Borg & Beck dry-plate, 11x7-inch disc clutch assembly is used for both 426 and 440 powerplants. It does a better-than-average job too, producing longer-than-expected service before needing a rest. Any clutch that'll continue to stick after 10 or 12 successive runs while a 490-lbs. ft. engine is thrashing against it can't be all bad. The Hurst linkage used here is a welcome addition to ease the shifting task.

An ad for the Charger.

If the photos suggest a rather high ground clearance here, it's due to the 15-inch wheels and F70 tires supplied with hemi-equipped Dodges. We also had a little trouble getting used to their appearance, but a good tire is worth a lot more than low riding height. Dropping the car is comparatively easy. Large-diameter front tires are no longer a drag racing speed secret, so they're worth having.

More than 2,500 miles of driving went by during our Charger time. Didn't mind a bit of it, either. So what about the trunk? It'll still hold a lot of wheat, right? Just pour it in. We may not be planning to buy a Charger 500, but it won't be because we don't like them. It has more to do with practicality. The older you get, the more practical you're *supposed* to be. Right now, we're busy makin' everybody see how practical we are. As soon as we've done that, we can go buy a hemi-engined something-or-other.

CYCLONE SPOILER

Hot Rod, September 1969

The Cyclones from Mercury should really stir things up for the high-performance-minded driver

After wandering around for a couple of years in search of a personality, the Montego is now at least getting a foothold in the U.S. auto scene, which is certainly not in need of further proliferation. Mercury's performance-character cars in their intermediate branch have received the Cyclone title. There's the regular Cyclone, the Cyclone GT, and the Cyclone Spoiler. All are very good-looking cars, coming off better in appearance than the Ford Division counterpart. There's no fastback offering on the '70 Cyclones, which may nullify the cars' use in Grand National racing. We wouldn't bet on that right now.

The NASCAR-born 429 HO engine is very much alive in the Cyclone option list. The Cyclone and the Cyclone Spoiler can be had only with 429-ci engines, in various power ratings, while the Cyclone GT comes with the newly designed 351-ci V-8 in two-barrel carburetor form. Upgrading to the four-barrel 351 is possible with the GT. The Cyclone and Cyclone Spoiler get the passenger car 429 V-8 in base form. The 10.5:1 compression, four-barrel Cobra Jet engine is the first option, and then the Ram-Air CJ, with a through-the-hood shaker air scoop, is the next step. Top of the list is the better-be-ready-for-action NASCAR 429, complete with aluminum heads, O-ring combustion chamber sealing, and a price tag which will most likely discourage all but the serious. Four-speed transmission cars get Hurst shifters, though not the linkage arms for the trans. That's not hard to change, and most likely will be done by knowledgeable owners. Suspensions equal the engines, with the competition package standard on Cyclone and Spoiler versions. A positive locking axle design is on the option list, and bias-ply fiberglass-belted tires are standard rigging for all Montegos.

Spoiler models are quite easily spotted by their front and rear air spoilers, and they have recessed instruments (tach, oil, temperature, and ammeter) in the center dash area. The gauges are optional for all 429 4V-engined cars.

The Cyclone may be a relatively big car, but it sure doesn't act like one. The tail end stayed well-glued to the asphalt during our sessions around the Dearborn ride and

During testing, the 1970 Montego Cyclone showed very few shortcomings.

Spoiler models have recessed instruments (tach, oil, temperature, and ammeter) in the center dash area.

The Cyclones from Mercury all are very good-looking cars, coming off better in appearance than the Ford Division counterpart.

The Cyclone may be a relatively big car, but it sure doesn't act like one. The tail end stayed well-glued to the asphalt during testing sessions around the Dearborn ride and handling course, and the front-end tire roll, while always evident, didn't get past the point of steering loss.

handling course, and front-end tire roll, while always evident, didn't get past the point of steering loss. The car will tilt and the tires will emit their peculiar noise, but if the throttle is used judiciously, there's no problem in negotiating tight turns. The 429 CJ engine held up under hours of this kind of treatment, though the tires did get a bit rounded. Hydraulic lifters are specified for all the 429s, including the NASCAR engine, but that may change by showroom introduction date.

Rear shocks are staggered, right ahead and left behind the axle, on four-speed cars. The 3:50:1 axle in the Cyclone we guided around the test track was suitable for road coursing, but barely got the car to the 100-mile-per-hour mark in the quarter. That's not bad for a big car, yet the optional 4.30:1 with Traction-Lok holds a lot of promise. Rear-wheel bounce was not evident on acceleration or deceleration.

Appearance-wise and performance-wise, there are very few shortcomings in Lincoln-Mercury division's most recent Montego.

MONTEGO CYCLONE, GT, & SPOILER

Wheelbase	117.0 in.
Tread: Front	60.5 in.
Rear	60.0 in.
Height	52.4 in.
Length	209.9 in.
Width	77.3 in.
Standard Engines	351-2V, Cyclone; 429-4V, GT & Spoiler
Optional Engines	429 CJ, CJ Ram-Air, and 429 NASCAR V-8
Body Style	2 dr. hardtop

THE HOT 70s SUPERCARS

STEVE KELLY
Hot Rod, October 1969

*If our initial look-see is any guide—and it usually is—1970 is
gonna be a good year for muscle cars*

AMERICAN MOTORS

American Motors President Roy Chapin claims AMC has "an affinity for cars that are fun to drive." Their small-sized cars—the Javelin, the AMX, and the new Hornet—meet this description very well, and each has a lot of personality. The Hornet, which replaces the Rambler (also known at one time as the American), exudes more personality than any domestic-made compact (or sub-compact, if you prefer). It's aimed for the under-$2,500 market, but thankfully can be ordered with a 304 V-8, SST optional trim, and performance-handling pieces. There'll be more meaty high-performance parts and options for the Hornet in the next few months, so we'll confine our discussion of the 179-inch-long car to endorsing it as being a very worthwhile automobile.

Both AMX and Javelin are 1.82 inches longer for '70, due to increased hood length. On optional high-performance–equipped models there are functional hood scoops, placed far enough forward to do some good, which induce cool air to the carburetor at about 80 percent throttle opening. Each car now has new interior appearance, including a new dash design. Only minor changes have been made to the exteriors.

Engine displacements have been revised upward, with the 290 V-8 now advancing to 304 cubic inches and a horsepower rating of 210. The 343 engine moves up to 360 cubic inches, with a two barrel–fed design rated at 245 horsepower, and the four-barrel engine delivers 290 horsepower. Stroke on both is now 3.44 inches, up from last year's 3.28 inches. Block height has been raised slightly to accommodate the longer stroke. The 390 V-8 hasn't been increased in size, although horsepower is 325 instead of last year's 315. All engines have new combustion chamber shapes and larger exhaust ports. Cylinder head bolts have been enlarged for better gasket life and retention. The forged steel rods on 390 V-8s have heavier center sections to preclude chance of breakage. Cast crankshafts are fitted to 304 and 360 engines, though the forged steel 390 crank (3.57-inch stroke) will fit. The 360 engine will fit next year's new NASCAR rules (366-ci maximum), and if SCCA

Javelin SST

Trans-Am limits go up, the 360 will be waiting. Engine changes for 1970 have been accomplished partly as a result of the company's involvement with Trans-Am racing during the past two years.

Front suspensions on all '70 AMC cars incorporate upper and lower ball joints (previously only one was used), and anti-dive geometry is built into the front suspension design (another result of T-A racing). None of this is unique, but it at least brings AMC up to date.

Fifteen-inch-diameter by seven-inch-wide wheels with E60-15 tires are available for AMX and Javelin. Assembly-line rear axle gears reach the 3.91:1 ratio for big-engined cars, with a 3.54:1 being an intermediate plateau.

BUICK

The only real muscle car in the Buick gymnasium is its GS series, named after a line once known as the Gran Sport. The basic GS is a 350-ci V-8–equipped coupe. The next up is the GS 455 coupe or convertible—with a very strong 455-ci V-8 rated at 350 horsepower—or the 360 with Stage I equipment. It is derived from the earlier 400/430-inch V-8 design that no longer exists. The GS seems to be the recipient of formerly good Riviera styling; the Riviera now suffers in styling and the GS has benefited.

Extensive rework has been done to both 350 and 455 engine designs. The big-bore block has had further internal modifications, though it looks identical to the 400/430 V-8 from the outside. A new lubrication system brings oil up from the hydraulic lifters through tubular pushrods and then into the hollow extruded steel and carbo-nitrated rocker shafts. Rocker arms are die-cast in a low-porosity aluminum alloy material. The rockers are retained on the shaft by small nylon buttons, eliminating need for spacer springs. Valve train weight and attending friction are substantially reduced with this assembly, but unfortunately it won't adapt directly to older engines. An enlarged main oil gallery reduces sudden pressure drop. Water pump seals are made of a ceramic material that resists corrosion and abrasion. On the 455, main bearing caps are deeper, and bolt design has been revised to allow better and more even torque application. Intake manifold bolts on the 455 are now 7/16-inch-diameter instead of the previous 3/8-inch, and the gasket between intake and cylinder head provides tighter sealing.

Crankshafts are basically the same on the 455 as on the 400/430 engines. Bore is now 4.31-inch (was 4.04 on the 400, 4.19 on the 430), and stroke remains the same at 3.90 inches. Cylinder head gaskets are of a steel composition.

Hornet SST

AMX

The 350 V-8 hasn't been refined to the same degree as the 455, but much has been done nevertheless. The two-barrel 350 has a larger carburetor and better intake manifold design, which results in its now having 30 more horsepower than the '69 two-barrel V-8 (260 vs. 230). There's now a four-barrel regular fuel 350 that produces more horsepower (285) than the 1969 premium fuel four-barrel (280 horsepower), but it doesn't come in the GS. The 350 four-barrel GS premium fuel V-8 has a 315 horsepower rating and 10.25:1 compression. The 455 has a 10.0:1 compression ratio in all stages.

A selection of manual three- and four-speed transmissions and Turbo Hydros can be fitted to GS and GS 455 cars. Axle ratios on assembly-line cars range from 2.93 (with air conditioning) to 3.23, 3.42, 3.64, and 3.91:1. Limited slip is optional all the way.

Fiberglass-belted tires are standard, wheel size is 14x4 inches. Variable-ratio power steering is optional, and this type car can use that option. A rear-suspension stabilizer bar (.875-inch-diameter) is optional, and substantially improves road behavior. Wheelbase and major body and chassis measurements are the same as in '69, with the exception that overall length has been reduced by more than an inch.

Total car design is exceptionally good. Functional air intake scoops in the hood are still standard and remain in a spot well removed from contact with high-pressure air current. That's about the most serious fault on the '70 Buick performer, which puts it high on the "good things" list.

CHEVROLET

The Chevrolet division's new car story for 1970 will come on in stages. Corvette introduction will be some time after the regular line showing, though it should take place within 1969. Camaro introduction is to be in January or February, but there will be a

Buick GS 455

Camaro offered up to that time. It will have the '69 shape and appearance, and there is really no model year assigned to the car that'll continue to grace showroom floors until the January-or-February new model. Now would be a perfect time to cut the price down on the '69-appearing Camaro. That might well be the plan. A couple of recent production line changes now make it possible to order a Z-28 Camaro with a Turbo Hydra-Matic, or—on special fleet order—a ZL-1 aluminum-block 427. The later-in-the-year Camaro, which is more of an advanced '71 model than a late '70, will feature these options, plus a couple of other exceptional performance aids that are now in the works. With this kind of news spreading around, it might require a healthy price cut on the current Camaro to keep it selling.

The Nova retains the same size it had in '69, and nearly the same exterior and interior appearance. Some slight trim reworking is all that has been done. A four-cylinder is still listed for powering Novas, as is a 230-ci and 250-ci six. There's a 307 V-8, and a pair of 350-ci V-8s, the four-barrel version (300 horsepower) available only in the coupe with SS equipment. Big-block 396 V-8s will continue to be optional in varying modes, or at least that is the plan.

The Chevelle is the only refined muscle car from Chevy that is relatively different from last year's and that will be ready on announcement day. Exterior and interior styling is changed a good deal, but the car is still easily recognizable as a Chevelle. Wheelbase remains at 112 inches for the coupe (116 for sedans), overall length is greater by .1-inch

Buick GS 455

(197.2 inches), width is less by .6-inch (75.4 inches), and both front and rear tread is 59.8 inches (an increase of .8-inch).

The SS 396 has gained even more distinction through the use of special trim markings and a domed hood. A cowl induction hood is optional for the SS 396. The 350-horsepower 396 V-8 is standard with the package, and either a four-speed or Turbo Hydro is available. There's an even larger displacement V-8 en route for the upper series Chevelles that should be able to do more than just hold its own with other powerplants, but release dates haven't been scheduled yet.

A 400-ci small-block V-8 is new for '70 with Chevelles, Chevrolets, and Monte Carlos. It develops 330 horsepower in its four-barrel carbureted production form. Bore/stroke measurements are 4.126 inches by 3.76 inches. There's also a regular-fuel 265-horsepower version of it for the bigger cars, and in both cases a cast-iron crank is

Chevelle SS 396

used. Bore spacing at 4.40 inches is the same as that in other Chevy small-blocks. A 454-ci big-block V-8 (option LS5) is offered for big Chevys, Monte Carlos, and Chevelles. Depending on where you look, the horsepower rating goes from 360 to 390. A 345-horse-power model (LS4) can be had in Chevrolets. Bore/stroke data is 4.251x4.00 inches, a forged steel crank is included, and bore spacing is 4.84 inches. Where the 454-inch engine is used, the 427 V-8 has been dropped.

Chevy's new car, the Monte Carlo, is by no means a muscular runner and is aimed at the higher-price market along the lines of the Grand Prix. It's on a 116-inch wheelbase and stretches out for 205.8 inches. Both measurements are less than on the GP. It comes only in a coupe body style with some type of V-8 (350, 400, or 454), and power front discs are standard.

CHRYSLER-PLYMOUTH

The Chrysler-Plymouth Division broke the mold for its "old" Barracuda—the carmaker now followed suit of other makers and turned its specialty car into a pony car. It isn't one bit shy on available performance equipment, and all of it is offered on an assembly-line-installation basis. The new body is shorter and wider than the earlier Barracuda, with the new one based on the intermediate Belvedere chassis. There are three models: Barracuda, Gran Coupe, and 'Cuda. Two body styles, coupe or convertible, can be had. The muscle car is the 'Cuda.

All 'Cudas will have 11-inch-diameter drum brakes, heavy-duty suspension, front sway bar, F70-14 tires, hood pins, 4-inch-diameter road lights with 90,000 candlepower (which should create havoc with California laws), simulated hood scoops, 11-inch-diameter centrifugal-action clutch, dual exhausts, special identification trim, and a front track measurement increased to 60.2 inches (as opposed to 59.7 inches for other Barracudas). Ironically, the plush Gran Coupe has a 61.3-inch rear track, while the 'Cuda has a 60.7-inch measurement, but larger rear tires can at least be fitted to the 'Cuda easily.

The Street Hemi is a regular-line option in '70, and this year it has hydraulic instead of solid lifters. Cam specs are basically the same as before. A fresh air-inducing

Nova SS

Chevelle SS 454

Plymouth GTX

"shaker" hood scoop/cleaner is part of the Hemi option, and optional for the 440 six-barrel engine. The six barrel hasn't been substantially changed for '70 from its '69 configuration, and it still carries a 390-horsepower figure. The four-barrel 440-ci V-8 is offered also, and so is the lightweight 340-ci engine. The 383 high-performance, four-barrel–equipped V-8 is the standard 'Cuda engine. Both the 440 and 426 must be ordered with either a four-speed manual (which features a new pistol grip on its Hurst linkage) or a three-speed automatic TorqueFlite. A floor-mounted three-speed stick, with forward speeds synchronized, is standard with 340 and 383 engines, though four-speed or automatic are optional. Rear gears start at 2.76 and progress to a 4.10:1 ratio, with limited-slip movement available.

A new model in the Valiant line for '70 is called the Duster, and it's right out of the Road Runner school of thought. Both a 198- and a 225-ci six, as well as a 318 V-8, are offered in the basic Duster, but there's a Duster 340 model for really pure performance. The bucket-seated Duster coupe is light in price and bulk, measures 188.4 inches overall, has a 108-inch wheelbase, and features tip-open rear side glass, just like the original Road Runner. The all-synchro three-speed is standard with the 340; four-speed or automatic are optional. The '69 Barracuda dash is used, and there are some pretty worthwhile dress-up and roadworthy options offered for Dusters.

Plymouth 'Cuda

Road Runner and GTX have received some noticeable outside styling changes but are otherwise the same as in '69. A new dashboard—the same type as seen in the Charger—is fitted to both models. A functional flip-open "air grabber" hood scoop, forward-mounted on the hood and vacuum-controlled by an inside lever, is standard with the hemi-engined Road Runner and GTX and optional with 383- and 440-powered cars. The 383 four-barrel V-8 continues as standard, with the two 440 V-8s and the hemi optional. That's about the way it was last year, and there's certainly no embarrassment connected with carrying this lineup over to '70. A 2.45:1 economy axle ratio can be ordered. The 3.23:1 ratio is the predominant standard ratio, but performance gears of 3.55:1, 3.91:1, and 4.10:1 are listed for assembly-line inclusion.

DODGE

The Dodge boys have learned car marketing and car building rather quickly in the past few years, and their current products show how well they did their homework. The newest car from Dodge is the Challenger, a car with a body shape that's neither bland nor controversial, yet incorporates many virtues overlooked by other small-car makers. It has a 110-inch wheelbase—two inches longer than the Barracuda—and is 191.3 inches in overall length. Height is 51.5 inches, rear track is 60.7 inches, and front is 59.7 inches. Width is 76.4 inches, which is only .3-inch less than a Charger. This means interior width is generous, too.

Valiant Duster

Plymouth Hemi 'Cuda

Challenger comes in coupe or convertible, and in two different series, Challenger and Challenger R/T. In both, the special edition comfort and appearance option can be ordered, but performance engines on the big end of the displacement scale come only in R/Ts. The 383 four-barrel V-8 is standard with R/T models, and the 340-ci engine can be ordered. The hydraulic lifter–outfitted 426 Street Hemi, with its pair of Carter four-barrel carbs, is production-line-available, as are the two 440-ci V-8s: the high-performance four-barrel variety and the triple Holley two-barrel inducted Six Pack. A domed hood with simulated scoops is found on all R/T models, though a through-the-hood "shaker" scoop with filter element is available for Hemi and 440 engines.

Chrysler Corporation's new all-synchromesh three-speed manual, using strut-type synchronizers and slotless synchro rings, is standard with 383 and 340 engines. The other R/T motivators must be ordered with a four-speed, Hurst-shifted transmission, or the three-speed TorqueFlite (offered with a ratchet shift mechanism in conjunction with center console). One thing about the Challenger is that a new console was designed for it, rather than have it make do with the "traditional" Mopar console that has outlived every other centerpiece design.

Dodge Challenger R/T

Dodge Charger

The Challenger series isn't a real lightweight, since it gets its chassis from the intermediate Coronet line. All R/T versions have heavy-duty underpinnings and a hefty front stabilizer bar. Wheel sizes go from 14-inch-diameter by 4.5-inch-width to 15x7. Bias-ply, fiberglass-belted tires are standard on all Dodges for '70. Rear-axle ratios reach 4.10:1 for production-built cars. Standard drums have an 11-inch diameter, and power front discs are extra-cost-available. Naturally, torsion bars are used up front, and semi-elliptic leaf springs are in back.

The Dart appearance is changed for '70, with the back body section getting the major rework. There are only three models now: the Dart, Swinger 340, and Dart Custom. The 340 is the biggest displacement V-8 available, and available only in the Swinger. Idle speed has been boosted to 800-1,000 rpm on the 340 to obtain lower emissions during idle and deceleration. Compression ratio is listed at 10.5:1, and horsepower rating should remain as it was in '69.

Super Bee appearance is changed quite a lot for the new year, but engine/transmission and basic running gear are carried over from '69. The Coronet R/T and the Super Bee both have hi-rise hoods, and fresh air scoops are optional. Standard in the Super Bee is the 383 four-barrel V-8, and the 440 four-barrel V-8 is standard in the Coronet R/T. The other Dodge muscle motors are optional for both cars.

Three Charger models are offered for '70: the Charger (with a 225-ci six or a 318 V-8), the Charger 500—not the special fastback-roof kind—(with 318, 383 three-barrel or four-barrel V-8), and the Charger R/T (which gets the 383 four-barrel V-8 standard and the 426 or 440 four-barrel or Six Pack at extra charge). A new grille is the most significant change, and it blends well with the rest of the body shape. The Six Pack 440, which incidentally has a cast-iron intake manifold for 1970, doesn't need a special hood when supplied in the Charger.

Dodge Dart Swinger

FORD

There's more than just revised sheet metal on Ford's Torino models for 1970 that sets them apart from the '69s. Wheelbase is longer by one inch (117 inches), and overall length is 5.1 inches greater. Most of this is in front overhang, which is 4.1 inches more than on last year's Torino. Height is reduced by 1.2 inches, the front end is lower and more pointed, and the windshield angle has been sloped six degrees more than on the '69. The car therefore has better air-cutting ability and greater potential for higher speeds—like when they're used in NASCAR Grand National racing. Front and rear tread width is wider by nearly two inches (60.5 inches front, 60.0 inches rear), as is overall width (76.7 inches).

The NASCAR-bred 429 Crescent head engine is offered with Torino Cobra fast-backs (the only body style now offered for Cobras) and will be available in limited quantities, but at least they will be assembly-line optional. It's titled the 429 4V Cobra Jet HO, and it includes the neat aluminum heads, 2.29-inch intake valves, 1.91-inch exhausts, magnesium rocker covers, forged crank and rods, mechanical lifter cam, 735 cfm Holley carb with manual choke, compression ratio of 10.5:1 (which might well be very honest), and a horsepower figure of 375. When ordered, this engine requires a good deal of other equipment on the car—like a four-speed transmission (now with Hurst shifter), 3.50 rear axle or lower (higher number), competition suspension, F-60 tires on 15-x-7-inch wheels, power front discs, power steering, and high-output electrical system. The HO 429 can also be ordered in Mustangs, in which case the battery is trunk-mounted and a hood scoop with manually operated valve is included, as well as power steering with external oil cooler and a front air dam/spoiler.

Torino Cobra

For the less-than-high-bank racer, there are three other 429 engines for Fairlane and Torino cars, but not for Mustangs. The HO is the only one offered there. The base 429 "C" engine has production wedge-head equipment, cast-iron crankshaft, 11.1 compression, hydraulic lifter camshaft, 700 cfm Rochester carb, and a horsepower rating probably around the 350 area. At this time, that information hasn't been made public. The next step up is fitting Cobra Jet equipment to this 429, which means a ram-air induction system with a shaker hood scoop.

The competition suspension package, standard with Cobras, features staggered rear shocks and higher rate springs, shocks, and front stabilizer. A rear stabilizer is now optional for Mustangs and very shortly will be available for all other Ford car models.

The Mustang will rely on 428-ci big-blocks in '70, with or without Cobra Jet pieces. Slight refinements have been made here, but they are still the basic engines used previously and continue with the 335 horsepower rating. The Boss 302 is very much alive too and can be had only on the fastback Mustang with Boss 302 items such as competition suspension, front air spoiler, and external trim distinction. The 390 isn't used in any of the muscle cars. A totally new 351-ci V-8, different from last year's small-block 351, is offered for most Mustangs and Torinos and can be either two- or four-barrel-carbureted. It has canted valves, 2.19-inch-diameter intakes and 1.71-inch exhausts, 1/2-inch-diameter main bearing bolts, round ports in the heads, and a heritage tracing right over to the 429. This new small-block 351 is called the Cleveland engine.

Mustang Boss 302

Drag pack options for either 428- or 429-engined cars bring with them a choice of 3.91 or 4.30 rear axles (with a new positive-action No Spin locker) and engine oil cooler; for the 429 alone, there's a mechanical valve lifter camshaft, 780 cfm Holley carb, high nodular iron crank, forged aluminum pistons, and four-bolt main caps on Nos. 2, 3, and 4 positions.

Mustangs have received only a token number of styling changes, which is for the best. Both Torino and Mustang will benefit more from mechanical changes this year than anything the reshaped sheet metal could ever do.

LINCOLN-MERCURY

The Cyclone Spoiler, even with its standard front and rear spoilers, and the Cyclone and Cyclone GT (derived from L-M's Montego) are better-looking than their '68-'69 ancestors, as well as the current Torino. The fastback isn't offered in the Cyclone body lineup, but that shouldn't matter. If Lincoln-Mercury dealers get their way (and they should), and Mercury nameplates continue to adorn some of the Ford Motor Company

Montego Cyclone Spoiler

factory Grand National cars with the first-time-ever factory-optional Crescent Head 429, Cyclones will most likely fare well after a little race car engineering is applied. The coupe roofline is pretty fast.

The Cougar didn't make out as well in the new-style department. If the additional "waterfall" center grille section had been left out, the car would look as good as it did last year, and that would be a compliment.

Both Cougar and Montego are longer in '70, 3.7 inches more on the Montego (209.9 inches overall), and 2.3 inches more for Cougar (196.1 inches), with the increase all in the front. Wheelbase is 117 on the Montego—an inch more than in '69. Overall width and tread measurements are greater on the Montego than they were previously. Both cars can be equipped with the 429 NASCAR engine, the Eliminator series only for Cougar, and any two-door hardtop for Montego. The Cyclone GT gets the new 351 two-barrel Cleveland V-8 as standard, and the Cyclone model has the 429 four-barrel V-8. The wedge-head 429s in the Cyclone series can be had with or without Ram-Air, which utilizes the then-functional hood scoop. The Ram-Air 429 is the base engine in the Cyclone Spoiler. No 428 or 390 V-8s are available. Hydraulic lifters are in all Lincoln-Mercury engines.

Close- or wide-ratio four-speed gearboxes are shown, with Hurst shifters included, and when the high-strength-component competition suspension is ordered, rear shocks are staggered to counteract wheel hop on acceleration and deceleration. This applies to the Cougar and Montego.

The Cyclone Spoiler and Cougar Eliminator have standard front and rear air spoilers. Cyclone Spoiler dash panels are fitted with necessary instrumentation in the center area. Both cars have tachometers, and the Eliminator has a 24-hour timepiece directly opposite the front passenger.

Engine availability in the Eliminator 351 four-barrel Cleveland standard; Boss 302 four-barrel CJ, with or without Ram-Air; and the limited-production 429 Crescent NASCAR V-8 all optional. Competition suspension (high-rate front and rear springs and shocks, front and rear stabilizer bar) is included on all Cougars with engines larger than 351 cubic inches.

A new positive-action No Spin locker-type rear axle is optional on nearly every Cougar or Montego model, including the 4.30:1 gear. On NASCAR 429-powered cars, 15-inch by 7-inch wheels are required.

As with most other cars for 1970, the L-M products will have high-back bucket seats, a locking steering column, and fiberglass-belted tires in all cases.

OLDSMOBILE

Oldsmobile is getting back where it once was and where it likely should be: innovators of workable and unusual equipment that generates high performance. The 442 is its only muscle car candidate and, as in the case of Buick, that may well be all Olds needs this year.

Montego Cyclone Spoiler

Cougars

Engine size is upped to 455 cubic inches (from the previous 400) on all 442 models, and the W30 option is the forced-air induction version. Base rating is 365 horsepower, and it's 370 for the W30. Cutlass and 442 series cars have the same wheelbase as the '68-'69s and are nearly the same in other areas of measurement. Performance will be where the advance shows the most.

All forced-air induction cars, the W30 and W31—the Cutlass "S" 350—will have fiberglass hoods with forward-mounted scoops providing outside airflow. "W" series engines in all car lines have aluminum intake manifolds. There's a W27 option for '70, which is an aluminum center section rear-end housing, finned for added cooling and refined for better lubrication. This in itself is quite a treat. A W25 option, which is just the forced-air induction components, is offered for any 442. "Conecc" rod bearings, a new idea that incorporates almost total concentric bearings rather than an eccentric shape, are in use in all engines. They have a slightly eccentric shape at the mating point between rod and cap but are otherwise concentric, which should improve oil pressure and oil flow. All engines feature rotating valves, an idea used for some time in trucks. The valve rotator, likened best to a one-way friction clutch, fits between spring and rocker. The valve turns two degrees during each opening and closing cycle. Advantages of this system are that the valve returns to a fresh seat every cycle, carbon deposits on the seat are minimized (if not eliminated) because of the constant polishing action, valve temperatures are more uniform, and valve life is lengthened considerably. TCS (transmission controlled spark) is

Oldsmobile 442

Oldsmobile 422

Oldsmobile 422

used in all '70 Oldsmobiles. It provides for spark advance only when the car is in high gear. This is a product of more stringent emission controls, and the final result is exhaust emissions reduced by as much as 30 percent. A switch senses the car's gear ratio, and no signal is sent to the vacuum-controlled advance until the high gear ratio is engaged. We don't know where the switch is, and furthermore, tampering with it is quite likely an offense that carries a heavy penalty.

Torque converters in automatic-transmissioned "W" cars now hold the engine speed at or near peak torque output longer, producing more tractive effort up to 30 miles per hour, the most critical period. Rear axle bearings are now roller-type, replacing the earlier ball-bearing design.

Manual disc brakes are standard (front only) on W30 and W31 Olds, with a new tandem booster power-assist optional. A link-type front stabilizer bar (.937-inch-diameter) and an .875-inch-diameter rear bar joining the lower rear control arms are included on 442 and W31. Variable-ratio power steering is a new and welcome option for all intermediate Oldsmobiles.

On top of all the good engineering technology applied to the '70 Olds performance vehicles, the Cutlass and the 442 are good-looking creations. Wishing Oldsmobile well for 1970 might be anticlimactic.

PONTIAC

Pontiac is restricted to only one supercar for regular 1970 model introduction, but since the GTO kicked off the entire Detroit-built chase to capture the always-spreading hot rod market, this is the one to have if it happens to be all you've got. This car still has the status and the sales to let it continue influencing the balance of the industry and, more important, potential customers.

The '70 Firebird, which is more like a '71 model being introduced early, won't premiere until January or February of 1970. Meanwhile, there will be the '69-shaped Trans-Am and/or regular Firebird models on display. Even this isn't for sure. There just might be a long dry spell until early 1970.

A 455-ci V-8 can be ordered with GTOs and Judges, but Ram-Air isn't part of the package. The mid-range torque (500 lbs. ft. @ 2,700 rpm) oversquare (4.152-inch bore x 4.220-inch stroke) has a 360-horsepower rating and uses a single Rochester four-barrel. The 350-horsepower 400-ci V-8 is the standard GTO power, and the 366 Ram-Air and 370-horse Ram-Air IV are continued options. Manual three-speed gearboxes are regularly fitted to the base engine, the 455 and the 400 Ram-Air. Either close- or wide-ratio four-speeds can be ordered with the base V-8 or the Ram-Air, but only close-ratio with the 455

Pontiac GTO

Pontiac GTO

and the Ram-Air IV. Turbo Hydro is an option on all of them. Rear gears from the factory reach a low of 4.33:1, and all ring gears are 8.125 inches in diameter except the 3.31:1, which is 8.875.

Standard wheel size is 14 inches by 6 inches, and tires are glass-belted G78-14. The only power brake offering with GTOs is front discs, which is as it should be.

A rear stabilizer bar—.875-inch-diameter in 1070 carbon steel—combines with the front link-type bar, measuring 1.125-inch-diameter of SAE 9260 steel, to increase roll stiffness. With the bars doing their stability work, spring rates have been reduced without any loss in handling ability, yet with a very noticeable increase in ride and road comfort. The latest GTO rides smoother than any previous edition, with substantially better handling traits. Stiff springs are on the way out.

GTO styling is about the best it has ever been, although it has never had any weak points. The front end now takes on a Firebird look, and Endura remains as the front bumper material. The back end slightly resembles the '68 Grand Prix, the last of the big-bodied GPs. Interior changes are primarily in the dash, which now has an engine-turned panel accenting the woodgrain trim. Most GM cars have their radio antennas imbedded in the windshield glass, pioneered last year on the GP, and the GTO is no exception. Overall length is 202.9 inches, a 1.7-inch increase over the '69. Width is .9-inch greater at 76.7 inches. Front and rear track are 61.0 inches and 60.0 inches, in that order.

The Judge GTO is still offered. It accounted for nearly seven percent of the total '69 GTO sales, despite its late introduction. Better figures are expected for the Firebird of 1970, which will also get a late start.

If anyone cares to know, the overhead cam six has been discontinued. A Chevy six replaces it in the six-banger models. How do you like that? Chevy buries a Corvair and inherits a new market for an in-line six.

MISTER MUSCLE OF 1970

STEVE KELLY
Hot Rod, November 1969

Buick's new GS 455 makes it hard to stay away from the muscle car mania

Buick may have the surprise issue in the supercar series this model year. The 400-ci engine in its GS series has been replaced by a 455-inch version, conservatively rated at 360 horsepower in Stage 1 dress. The standard GS 455 engine has a 350 rating, and both figures are taken at 4,600 rpm. Torque is 510 lbs. ft. at 2,800 rpm on both 455s. Combined with the new powerplant is one of the most eye-appealing exterior shapes this car has ever had, and it may qualify as the best-looking intermediate and/or muscle car of the season.

The auto-buying world may not be ready for—or in need of—plus-400-ci V-8–engined supercars, but that's gradually becoming the only size to be offered in the identity-laden performance cars. Time will have to be the judge as to whether or not this is the proper direction for U.S. automakers to be heading.

Cylinder bore is 4.3125 inches in the new 455, versus 4.040 in the earlier 400-inch V-8. Bore-spacing is the same at 4.750 inches. Stroke is also the same between 400 and 455: 3.90 inches. The 455 is derived directly from the 1967-introduced, wedge-shaped combustion chamber engine. Cast aluminum alloy pistons, forged rods, and a nodular iron crank (with the same journal diameter size as a 400-incher) make up the lower end. Compression ratio is 10.0:1 for both regular GS 455s and Stage 1 models. A single Rochester Quadrajet is used on all GS engines. The 350-horsepower camshaft readings are identical to 455 V-8–powered LeSabre and Wildcat Buicks, though in those cars the same engine carries a 370-horsepower rate, and with the same torque figure. Wonder who's running their dyno! These specs are: Intake opens 17 degrees BTC, closes 93 degrees ABC for a 290 degree duration; exhaust opens 93 degrees BBC, closes 49 degrees ATC, for a duration of 322 degrees. Valve opening overlap is 66 degrees. Lift at the valve is .3891-inch on the intake, and .4602-inch on the exhaust. Hydraulic lifters are used, and 1.60:1 ratio rocker arms are fitted. The higher rpm range Stage 1 cam specifications are: Intake opens 28 degrees BTC, closes 108 degrees ABC, with a duration of 316 degrees; exhaust opens

This is a comfortable car, especially from an enthusiast's viewpoint. It is quiet-running and carries outside styling that surpasses the majority of the current crop of muscle machines.

at 98 degree BBC, closes 62 degree ATC; 2.13-inch intake and 1.755-inch exhaust. No significant change is made to the lifters or rockers with Stage 1 pieces.

The Stage 1 option consists of low-restriction dual exhausts, high-rpm-operation valve train, a special hydraulic lifter cam, revised oil pump, 3.64:1 ratio limited-slip axle, and higher shift-point automatic transmission, when the Turbo Hydro is ordered.

External appearance of a 455 is no different from a 400/430 design, but changes within the bigger displacement block render it quite different from the early engine. Main bearing caps have deeper sections, and main bolts have been altered for easier servicing. An enlarged main oil gallery reduces chance of the crankshaft drying out at high rpm, with subsequent bearing damage now being less of a risk. Stage 1 V-8s have a 60 psi oil pump regulator spring, versus the normal 40 psi. The new valve gear takes oil from the hydraulic lifters and passes it up through the tubular pushrods to the new pattern rocker arms. The rockers are low-porosity, pressure die-cast aluminum, retained on carbo-nitrided, extruded rocker shafts by small nylon buttons. Steel composition head gaskets are new to this engine, as are 7/16-inch intake manifold bolts, replacing the older, 3/8-inch cap screws. Water pump seals are now produced from an extremely hard, smooth ceramic material that resists corrosion and abrasion. Most of the new pieces

The GS 455 styling adds to its appeal. The big V-8 ran well in desert tests and delivered acceptable fuel mileage.

won't adapt directly to 400/430-ci Buick engines, but mounting points on the 455 are exactly the same, making a transplant of this engine to earlier chassis very easy.

Our testing was conducted in the hot Arizona desert, near Mesa. Despite the 100-degree temperature, the near-4,000-pound coupe performed without complaint. The GS 455 ran below the 14.5-second quarter-mile clocking as soon as I discovered the automatic selected the optimum shift points better than I could do it manually. On earlier runs, my shifting was made at the 5,500-rpm mark, which means the shifts actually occurred at 5,600-5,700 rpm due to the slight lag between lever movement and trans action. This proved too far past the power curve to suit the totally stock engine. The revised Turbo Hydro with Stage 1 Buicks has shift points set at 5,300 rpm for both upshifts, and that's exactly where it should shift with the stock setup. The car dropped to 14.4-second quarter-miles with the lever in "D" and my foot hard to the firewall. All runs were made with two people aboard, and the 14.4 times (and there were many of them) proved this car was quicker than some early-model street hemis tested in exactly the same trim. The car is surprisingly close to current showroom-fresh hemi Mopars, though it does have the benefit of 29 more cubic inches. A '69 GS 400 tested in our June 1969 issue, after receiving a liberal amount of handiwork and equipment, produced 12.7-second estimated times;

Hood scoops nestle neatly in sheet metal, but they're in the wrong spot for grabbing a heavy stream of air.

Twin snorkels on big Quadrajet air cleaner feed cool air from the functional hood scoops. The compartment gets rather crowded with air conditioning installed. Chrome rocker covers are standard.

and an identical four-speed GS 400 ran very low 12-second quarters. The same treatment to a GS 455 will certainly obtain high- or mid-11-second clockings.

A 3.64:1 limited-slip rear gear (the standard item) was in this car. Certain assembly-line GS models can be ordered with a 3.91 cog, and non-Stage 1 455 supercar intermediates receive a 3.42 ratio. G78-14 wide-pattern tires on six-inch rim width wheels are standard, and while they don't bolster quarter-mile speeds, they do contribute to making this a good-handling car. H78 and G70 profile tires are optional. The G78s on the rear did aid initial acceleration, though the relatively high stall speed of 1,500 rpm can cause the rear wheels to slip if full stall is exercised. Driving out from a lower speed, around 1,000 rpm, resulted in a more constant low-end pull and shorter time on the clocks.

Front disc brakes are optional for GS Buicks, and this is a recommended option. It's not that the 9.5-inch-diameter finned drums are no good, it's just that the disc option with a power booster is so

The interior layout is very much like a luxury-model Buick's. Full instrumentation is optional and recommended. Noise transfer to passenger compartment is at a very low level.

much better. This car had drums, and no fault was found there, but there's nothing like front calipers for repeated straight-line stops.

Car length is shorter by 1.3 inches for 1970, though front overhang is greater. Handling traits are even better than before. A linkless-design rear stabilizer (which has been optional for more than a year on the GS) was fitted to this one. It has a 7/8-inch diameter, and connects each lower rear control arm with the cross section fitted firmly against the underside of the rear-end housing. There's a bigger one up front and the combination of the two gives excellent handling to the coil-sprung car. This setup makes a coil suspension behave properly during twisty-road driving. Stiffer shocks would aid good handling, though hampering normal ride softness.

Variable-ratio power steering is the only soft-touch steering option. It adds much to front-end control, and when used in any GM intermediate, it brings the steering back to a closer relationship with the front wheels. "A" body cars have their linkage mounted forward of the front wheels, which sometimes causes the steering to be controlled as much by the front wheels as by the linkage. This isn't dangerous, considering that a driver is supposed to have his hands on the wheel, but the variable-ratio system gives more precise control from the steering wheel than previously possible. Gear ratio is 16:1 for the period of plus-or-minus four degrees of pitman arm travel, and this advances (or reduces) to 12.4:1 ratio by the end of the arm travel. Low-speed directional change therefore receives

Overall roadability is excellent in the Buick GS 445. A rear stabilizer bar contributes to this Buick's agile ways.

more assist, and sharp turns get less help. Getting the wheels off center is the biggest task, and here variable ratio proves its worth.

Interior styling is brightened by a new dash treatment similar in concept to the big Buick's. Bucket seats and a console are available, though the bench seat feels fine. Buckets do offer more leg support because the rounded backrest allows you to sit deeper in the seat. Warning lights are normally fitted to the panel, and full instrumentation can be included for an extra amount. A collapsible spare is optional.

Arizona's desert heat proved the value of the semi-closed cooling system included now on all Buicks. A translucent catch-can receives overflow, and this coolant is later drawn back into the radiator by a vacuum force that occurs after the engine has been shut down. This also provides for fluid level checks without removing the radiator cap. Had it not been for this feature, the GS 455 probably would've left all of its coolant on the desert floor. It left a healthy amount anyway.

An evaporative emission-control system is part of all California-sold '70 Buicks (and all other brands too). The fuel tank is closed off, and gas fumes are captured in a carbon canister and subsequently fed into the engine during operation. All '71 cars will have this.

Every GS-series Buick has fresh-air intake scoops in the hood. While they look great, they're placed too low and too far back to be able to capture the mainstream of passing air. Despite the disadvantage, these hood scoops are better than none at all.

All aspects of this car's performance, ranging from low-speed meandering to high-speed full-throttle enduros, were pleasing and satisfactory. It is a comfortable car, especially

ENGINE

Type	OHV V-8
Cylinders	8
Bore & Stroke	4.3125x3.90 in.
Displacement	455 ci.
Compression ratio	10.0:1
Horsepower	360 @ 4,600 rpm
Torque	510 lbs. ft. @ 2,800 rpm
Valves:	
Intake	2.125-in. dia.
Exhaust	1.750-in. dia.
Camshaft:	
Lift	.490-in.
Duration	316°
Overlap	90°
Rocker arm ratio	1.60:1
Tappets	Hydraulic
Carburetion	Single Rochester Quadrajet; vacuum-actuated secondary opening. 1.375-in.-dia. primary bores; 2.250-in.-dia. secondaries
Exhaust	Dual; low-restriction-type system

TRANSMISSION

Type	3-speed Turbo Hydra-Matic automatic, THM 400. Three-element torque converter; 2.05 maximum ratio at stall
Ratios: 1st	2.48:1 (42.5 mph @ 5,000 rpm)
2nd	1.48:1 (70.0 mph @ 5,000 rpm)
3rd	1.00:1 (105 mph @ 5,000 rpm)

DIFFERENTIAL

Type	Salisbury hypoid; semifloating axle shafts. Limited-slip with Stage 1 package
Ring gear diameter	8.50 in.
Final drive gear ratio	3.64:1

BRAKES

Type	Power-assisted drum type; finned aluminum front drums; composite cast-iron finned rear drum
Dimensions	9.5-in.-dia.
Total swept area	268.6 sq. in.
Effective area	152.0 sq. in.
Percent brake effectiveness, front (based on wheel cyl. size)	62.4%

SUSPENSION

Front	Independent with coil springs and ball joint Spring rate: 410 lbs.-per-in.
Rear	One-piece rear housing with coil springs (122 lbs.-per-in. rate) and upper and lower torque arm location
Shocks	Direct-acting tubular; 1.0-in.-dia. piston
Stabilizer: Front	Link type, .970-in.-dia.
Rear	Linkless, .875-in.-dia.
Tires	G78-14 wide-pattern, fiberglass-belted
Wheel rim width	6.0 in.
Steering:	
Type	Variable-ratio, power-assist, Saginaw; recirculating ball nut
Gear ratio	16.1:1 in center; 12.4:1 at ends of travel
Overall ratio	18.7:1 in center; 15.4:1 at ends of travel
Turning circle:	39.9 ft., curb to curb
Wheel diameter	16.0 in.
Turns lock to lock	4.06

PERFORMANCE

Standing start quarter-mile (2 aboard)	14.40 sec., 96 mph
0-30 mph	2.7 sec.
0-45 mph	4.5 sec.
0-60 mph	6.4 sec.
0-75 mph	9.4 sec.
40-60 mph	3.1 sec., 226.9 ft.
50-70 mph	3.5 sec., 308 ft.

FUEL CONSUMPTION

Best reading	14.9 mpg
Poorest	10.6 mpg
Average	12.5 mpg
Recommended fuel	Premium

DIMENSIONS

Wheelbase	112.0 in.
Front track	59.4 in.
Rear track	59.0 in.
Overall height	53.4 in.
Overall width	75.6 in.
Overall length	200.7 in.
Shipping weight	3,582 lbs.
Test weight	3,908 lbs.
Body/frame construction	Separate. Perimeter-type frame
Fuel tank capacity	20 gal.

from an enthusiast's viewpoint, quiet-running, and carries outside styling that surpasses the majority of our current crop of muscle machines. Now, if the Flint, Michigan, group is as sharp in marketing as it has proved to be with engineering, a lot of hot rodders who appreciate good cars could be driving GS 455s before the year is over.

JUST IN TIME

STEVE KELLY
Hot Rod, February 1970

The '70-Plus Firebird is ahead of its time—which only means the car is now what it should have been from the beginning

Pontiac calls its latest Firebird a '70-plus, although it is truly the '71 car advanced to a midyear introduction. The real '70 model was canceled after Bunkie Knudsen resigned at General Motors and took up employment with Ford, carrying with him all the knowledge of what the '71 Firebird and Camaro would look like. Chances of what Pontiac will call the '71 Firebird actually differing from the car shown on these pages is very slight.

Pontiac and GM styling have successfully bridged a long open breach between European styling and U.S. functionality with the Firebird. It has vinyl upholstery to guard against sloppy kids, and legroom for well-nourished American drivers, though not enough headroom for a Midwesterner who still wears his hat while driving, nor enough rear seat room to comfortably accommodate anyone over 12 years of age.

The latest Firebird appears smaller than earlier models because of its single side glass. It really is 1.2 inches longer than a 1969 'Bird, though it is a half-inch narrower. Wheelbase is the same as it has always been, but front and rear wheels have been moved forward three and a half inches relative to the body positioning. Overall height is greater now by a little less than one inch, which shows up in better front seat head and shoulder room, but the fastback roofline has really reduced rear seat room. Front seat adjustment on the '70 is excellent, eliminating one complaint of ours about the '67-'69 cars. Only a hardtop coupe is offered, and it can be had in four different versions: Firebird, Esprit, Formula 400, and Trans Am.

The base Firebird has a six-cylinder 250-ci Chevy engine, and the Esprit has a 350-inch V-8. The standard Formula 400 car has a 330-horsepower V-8, and the Ram-Air engine, with 345 horsepower, is optional. The Ram-Air engine is standard in the Trans Am, but it uses a through-the-hood scoop with the opening facing rearward, rather than using the regular ram-air scoops, which are formed in the Formula 400 fiberglass hood.

The Trans Am wears a front air dam and wheel house and a rear deck spoiler.

Handling and ride are the most significant aspects of the '70 Firebird. Ride is generally smoother and softer on all models because of reduced spring rates and the fact that the driveshaft tunnel in the rear is higher, which allows more suspension travel.

All cars have a .620-inch rear stabilizer bar, attached by a strut to the body and hooked to the rear housing at the spring/shock plate. It is insulated in rubber and causes no ride resistance, yet it really keeps the car in line and very level during cornering. The front stabilizer bar is a 1.00-inch diameter on standard cars, 1.125-inch diameter on 400-ci-powered cars, and a 1.250-inch size on the Trans Am. Spring rate at the front wheels is 75 pounds per inch on standard cars and 82 pounds on big-engined models, both of which are less than comparable '69 models. Rear spring rates are 91 pounds per inch on standard, with 105 and 126 being the rate on cars with big engines and/or heavy-duty suspension options. Alternate rate springs will be used, depending on the completed weight of the car, and

The engine sits well back on the chassis on all models.

The interior is both functional and attractive. The Formula steering wheel is boss.

staggered rear shocks are fitted to firm-ride and handling option–equipped Firebirds.

Combined with variable-ratio power steering and the relatively small-diameter and thick-rimmed Formula steering wheel, driver control, and ease of maneuverability is very much improved over any previous Firebird offering. Front and rear tread width is wider on V-8 Firebirds than before, now being 61.6 inches front and 60.3 inches rear. They used to be 60 inches at both ends, and with the narrower body width and increased tread, this Firebird is a handler.

Engines haven't been changed to any great degree. The Formula 400 without functioning air scoops ran 15.0s in the quarter, when hooked to a three-speed Turbo Hydro and 3.31 rear gear. That's with two passengers and a curb weight of 3,815 pounds wet. A 3.55 and a 3.73:1 are offered, as is a 4.10:1, for special applications. The 4.10 isn't generally installed at the factory. With functioning fresh-air scoops and a lower gear, there should be no trouble in making the Formula 400 run mid-14-second quarter-miles. The Trans Am Firebird we drove at the introduction session had one of last year's 3.90:1 gear sets and a close-ratio four-speed, which is a special order item only with 3.73 gearing on Formula 400 and Trans Am cars. Don Evans, slick-shifting editor of *Hot Rod*, did the driving honors here, bringing the Trans Am through the quarter-mile in 13.9 seconds at a speed of 102 miles per hour. Average elapsed time on the Trans Am was 14.00 seconds, a clocking that Don achieved four consecutive times.

The engine is good for 6,000 rpm but ran better when shifted at 5,500 rpm. Initial acceleration started from 2,000 rpm, giving the tires enough torque to light up just enough to keep the engine working and pulling evenly off the line. No trouble was encountered with either the Hurst shifter or the 10.4-inch clutch. It would be nice to have the shifter farther back on the tunnel, in a manner such as used on Corvettes, but Steve Malone, Pontiac's chief engineer, explains that it would require an additional linkage hookup. Still, it's worth looking into; the shifter would then be more convenient.

Ring gear diameter is 8.125 inches on 350 V-8–engined cars and under, and 8.875 inches with 400 V-8s. Naturally, limited slip is optional. The three-speed manual gearbox on 400s has a 2.42:1 low and a 1.58:1 second gear, and the widespread-ratio four-speed carries a 2.52 low, 1.88 second, and 1.46:1 third gear. The optional close-ratio has 2.20:1, 1.64:1, and 1.28:1 gearing. The Turbo Hydro isn't spread too badly, with a 2.48 first and 1.48 second. Shifters on automatic three-speeds can be ordered with the Rallye feature, allowing positive stops on upshifts.

There are a lot of things about the '70 Firebird that make it a car that's fun to run. Driver vision is better than expected from such a low car, mostly because the windshield is rounded rather high into the roofline. Side glass extends well back into the rear compartment, as does the entire door, to make rear seat access easy, and the rear glass doesn't cut out backside vision because the fastback roof lets the rear window top run quite high into the roof. Interior comfort is good, and the dash panel is laid out logically. Instrument panel access is a big point on the new Firebird. The gauge cluster is removed from the front after five screws are removed, and a panel below the steering column is held in by a pair of quarter-turn screws that can be slipped out to gain access to all panel lighting and the speedometer cable. A Rallye gauge package (option) includes a tachometer and clock in the left-side cluster.

Only bucket seats are offered in front, and they're not the high-back type. GM has elected to supply adjustable headrests rather than a high backrest because the carmaker feels the latter makes rear seat occupants feel cramped and reduces rearward vision from the front. Rear seats share a common bench-type backrest and have individual cushions.

There's not much we can say about the styling. Pictures do a better job. It is clean of gimmicks and there's not much in the way of protrusions to cause wind noise. The GTO-like front end is an Endura, the same as Pontiac's standard bearer. Unfortunately, single headlights have been substituted in place of the previous two-per-side, which probably is the result of an accountant's pen and a stylist's pencil.

How the racers will take to the new Firebird is yet to be seen. Pony car customers— and there are a lot of them—should be drawn to it in good numbers. The market is getting crowded now, and it will take a car at least as good as this one to keep Pontiac involved.

Rounded sheet metal flares out to cover wide tires.

PONTIAC FIREBIRD FORMULA 400

ENGINE ... 400-ci V-8, 4.1200-in. bore, 3.750-in. stroke, 330 hp @ 4,800 rpm, 430 lbs.-ft. torque @ 3,000 rpm. 10.25:1 compression.

CARBURETION ... Single Rochester 4-barrel Quadrajet

VALVE TRAIN ... Hydraulic lifters, 1.5:1 rocker arm ratio, 2.110-in. intake valve head diameter, 1.770-in. exhaust. Cam timing: 273... intake duration, 289... exhaust duration, 54... overlap. Lift at valve: .410-in. intake, .413-in. exhaust.

DRIVE TRAIN ... Turbo Hydra-Matic 3-speed automatic. 2.30:1 maximum ratio at stall. Semifloating hypoid pinion and ring gear. 8.875-in.-dia. ring gear. 3.31:1 final drive ratio.

BRAKES ... Front disc/rear drum with integral power assist. Nonassisted front discs standard. 10.94-in.-dia. front rotor, 9.5-in. rear drum. 52.6% front brake effectiveness.

WHEELS & TIRES ... 14-in.x7-in. steel wheels; F78-14 bias-belted standard, F70-14 standard with Trans Am and 400 sports option.

SUSPENSION ... Front: Independent with coil springs and direct-acting, 1.0-in. piston, firm control shocks. Link-type 1.125-in.-dia. alloy steel stabilizer bar. Rear: Hotchkiss drive, multileaf springs. Direct-acting tube shocks, staggered arrangement left to right. .620-in. dia. rear stabilizer.

STEERING ... Saginaw variable-ratio (optional) integral power assist. 14.0-in.-dia. wheel. Gear ratio: 14.5-11:1; overall: 16.0-12.1:1. 2.5 turns lock to lock.

PERFORMANCE ... Quarter-mile (best): 15.0 sec., 93 mph, Formula 400. Trans Am: 13.9 sec., 102 mph (345-hp Ram-Air and 4-speed close-ratio).

DIMENSIONS ... Wheelbase: 108.0 in.; front track: 61.6 in.; rear track: 60.3 in.; overall height: 50.4 in.; overall width: 73.4 in.; overall length: 192.3 in.; test weight: 3,815 lbs. (2,150 lbs. front, 1,665 lbs. rear); body/frame construction: integral with separate ladder-type front frame section; fuel tank capacity: 19.5 gal. (17.0, Calif. cars).

TOO MUCH OF
A REBEL

STEVE KELLY
Hot Rod, February 1970

*The ingredients are all there, but AM's "Machine" is not the
supercar it might've been*

AMC's Rebel Machine reminds us of a great defense lawyer who, despite losing his
biggest case, still boasted that it was his greatest courtroom scene. The Rebel
Machine is a good effort on American Motors' part, but it isn't a winner. If there's an
attempt being made here to chase down the well-known middle-class supercar market
with The Machine, nobody but American Motors need worry. Here's a car that lists for
around $3,500 at the starting point, but lacks an appealing interior, feels way too big
(and is) to be a handler, and is marked with more identity than Peter Fonda's two-
wheeler, with about the same taste. Not many of the folks we talked with while we had
the car could think of any reason they'd want this car, with 36 months to pay and all
the bright paint. Credit is due AMC for moving toward boosting the Rebel; maybe they
moved too far.

The Machine's 390 engine is given a rating of 340 horsepower, whereas other four-barrel 390-ci AM V-8s are rated 325 horsepower. The added 15 horsepower is said to be a
result of modified intake and exhaust manifolds. A box-type hood fixture incorporates a vacuum-operated fresh-air inlet to the carburetor. It also contains a hood-mounted tachometer
upon which little value can be placed. Its functionality in this spot is questionable. When
you're driving into the sun, the tach face can't be seen because of backlighting and dash-
top reflection into the windshield. When the sun is behind you, it quite often shines into
the tach, and its glass covering reflects the sun into your eyes. At night, the trouble with it is
that the light inside is at the top. It should be on the bottom and closer to the dial face and
needle. Neither the hood scoop nor the tachometer interferes with forward vision. Seating
position is high enough to overcome any difficulty here.

Exhaust report is somewhat impressive at idle, but any noise from the twin exhausts
hinting of a short-duration, high-lift cam is only that: a hint. The Machine's cam isn't
changed from the stock 390 cam, which has .457-inch valve lift on both intake and
exhaust and 266 degree duration on both. A dealer-available high-performance cam is

Ground clearance is too great on the Rebel "Machine." The bright stripes are $75 extra.

listed, but the factory can't put it in because it would mean an extra emission control certification, and the hi-perf cam probably won't pass that. It has .477-inch lift and 302 degree duration. Hydraulic lifters and 1.6:1 rockers are used throughout. The engine is good for around 5,000 rpm, yet the secondaries on the Carter-made four-barrel don't open soon enough (in stock form) to allow proper use of low- and mid-range torque. When they do open, the engine is near the shift point. The parts-counter AM cam will spin to 6,000 rpm, providing the full cam kit has been installed, which brings with it a decent set of valve springs and dampeners to properly keep the valves in motion. Either stock or with the optional cam from a dealer, the carburetor should be richened on the primary side and the secondaries fixed to open a bit sooner.

The shifter is about the only thing that could stand improvement on the four-speed gearbox. The handle is the same length as that used in the AMX and Javelin, which isn't too handy for a tall driver in a car with high seating like the Rebel. I like short shift handles, but this one's about two inches too close to the floor. The Hurst shifter should have received more attention during installation to prevent it from being too stiff, like the one in this test subject. A three-speed automatic may be ordered, although the four-speed is standard.

Over-the-road handling is better than might be expected from such a tall car, yet it still wants to shift too much weight to the wrong side. A .95-inch-diameter rear sway bar

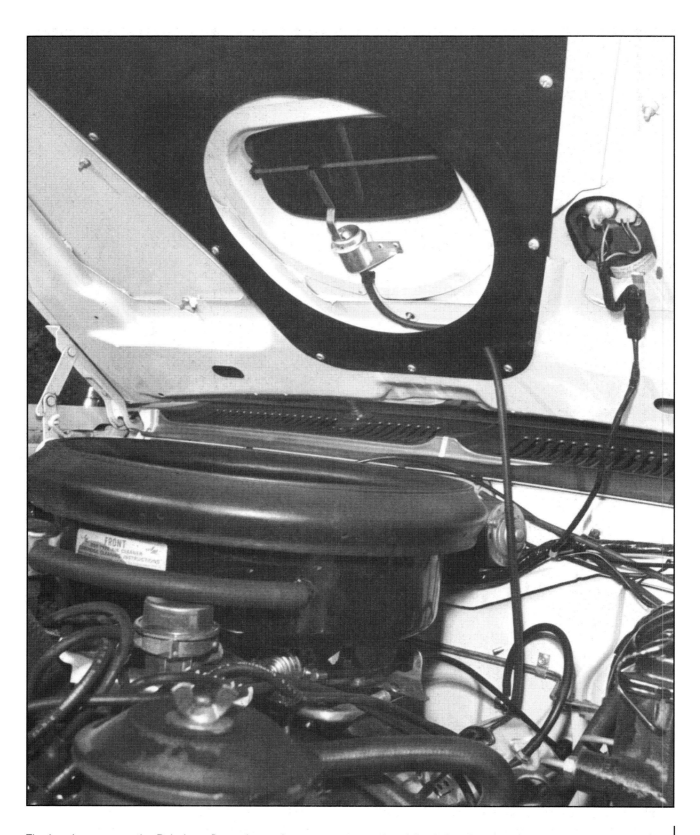

The hood scoops on the Rebel are flapped open by a vacuum control and feed directly to carburetor.

Tach is hard to read in this location, and rather optimistic with an eight-grand scale.

is tied to the rear end, and heavy-duty (125-pounds-per-inch wheel rate) coil springs are used at the rear. The front end has coils also, 141-pound wheel rate, and a .94-inch stabilizer. All this sounds good, and it would be good if the car were about a foot lower. Variable-ratio power steering is almost mandatory. The manual control box has a mere 6.0 turns lock to lock. The power assist is only 3.2 turns.

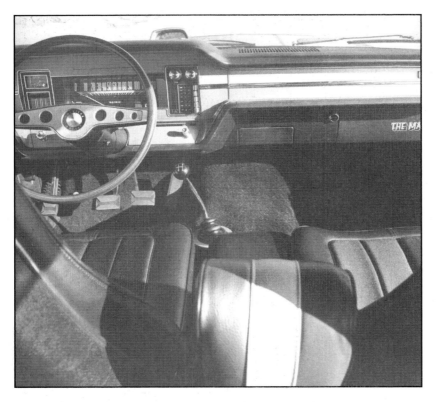

The dash is too blank. In the words of one viewer: "Looks like a taxi."

When testing the 1970 AMC Rebel, weight shift to the rear on acceleration startup, and upon upshifting, was severe.

The standard rear axle carries a 3.54:1 ratio, with a 3.15 gear offered with automatics. A 3.91:1 ratio and limited slip are optional. The Machine we tested had the 3.91, a pretty good compromise gear. Wheels are seven inches wide and have a unique trim ring that is pressed onto the rim. While it looks good, it won't snap off, and it prevents installation of most tire-wheel balancers. The tires are E60-15 Goodyears, and the spare is a collapsible one. The fold-up spare in this trunk makes the luggage compartment a guest room. Brakes on The Machine are excellent. Bendix front discs with power assist are mated with 10-inch-diameter rear drums, also power-assisted. These brakes and the big tires really draw the car down to zero in a hurry. Gives you lots of time to look in your rear view and pray that the poor guy behind you can do as well.

Clutch pedal linkage is long, which is good, since the car needs gentle take-off procedures to get it under way through a quarter-mile. The long clutch travel is disconcerting on upshifts, however, and you've got to remember to bring your left foot way up when engaging the clutch. Power shifts help, naturally, but they don't help the rear end. By the time we got this Rebel, the bushings in the rear control arms had been worn loose by quite a few earlier quarter-mile runs. Weight shift to the rear on acceleration startup, and upon upshifting, is severe. The answer to it is stiffer rear shocks and/or Air Lifts to support the tail end. The problem would become serious if slicks were used.

Best time possible over the Irwindale quarter-mile surface, which exhibited "super bite" the day we ran, was 14.49 seconds at 93.00 miles per hour. Can't say this is all bad for such a boxlike front-ended car, but dropping the car closer to the ground (that ought to stir up a little correspondence from the lift-kit makers), richening the carburetor, bumping the ignition lead a couple of notches, and adding stiffer rear shocks ought to bring this near-4,000-pound car close to 14 seconds even. Now if this performance was coupled with a more sedate-appearing vehicle, though one not devoid of personality, there'd be a greater chance of this AM product providing easy sales for dealers. As it appears, floor traffic will be good, mostly because of its presence there. The amount of sales generated by it could show up more with other AMC models than with The Machine. Of course if this should happen, then the car is a success from the corporation's viewpoint. The Machine is going to be offered in 14 different colors, with or without a tar-paper (vinyl) roof. Hoods on succeeding models will be flat black finished with silver accents. This exterior availability sounds better and more liveable. All interiors have high-back bucket seats upholstered in pure vinyl, carpeting and a special woodgrain-rimmed wheel with rim-blow honker. There's plenty of space within, though the rear seat headroom is scant for six-foot and taller passengers.

It's not pleasant to see anyone or anything fail. Hope we don't see that in The Machine. It may prosper as an effective sales tool in the showroom, but this isn't planned as a limited-edition car. It'll be here for some time. An early proposal within the AMC workings featured the Hornet as the subject of a nearly identical undertaking. The Hornet would've been the wiser choice, but the Rebel got the strongest vote. Someday, if things don't go right, impeachment proceedings may be instituted.

AMC REBEL MACHINE

ENGINE ... 390-ci V-8. 4.17-in. bore x 3.57-in. stroke. 340 horsepower @ 5,100 rpm, 430 lbs.-ft. torque @ 3,600 rpm, 10.0:1 compression ratio.

CARBURETION ... Model OWM4 single four-barrel, 1.56-in. pri., 1.69-in. sec.

VALVE TRAIN ... Hydraulic lifters, 1.6:1 rocker arm ratio. 2.025-in.-dia. intake valve, 1.625-in. exhaust. Cam timing: 266° duration, intake & exhaust, 38° overlap. Lift at valve: .457-in. intake & exhaust.

DRIVE TRAIN ... Manual 4-speed transmission. Ratios:1st, 2.23:1; 2nd, 1.77:1; 3rd, 1.35:1, 4th, 1.00:1. Borg & Beck semi-centrifugal clutch, 10.5-in. dia. Dana, live-axle, one-piece housing, 8.88-in. ring gear diameter and limited-slip differential. 3.91:1 final drive ratio.

BRAKES ... Bendix front disc/rear drum, integral single-diaphragm vacuum power booster. 11.19-in.-dia. rotor, 10.0-in. rear drum, 104.9-sq.-in. effective area.

WHEELS & TIRES ... 15-in.x7-in. steel wheels; E60-15 fiberglass-belted tread tires

SUSPENSION ... Front: Independent unequal-length upper & lower arms, twin ball joints, lower arm strut rod. Coil spring & shock on upper arm, 1.19-inch shock piston; .94-in. 1040 steel stabilizer bar. Rear: 4-link (control arms) with coil springs. 1.19-in.-dia. piston shocks, frameless-type 1090-grade steel .95-in.-dia. stabilizer.

STEERING ... Saginaw, recirculating ball, variable-ratio gearbox with integral rotary valve. 16-in.-dia. wheel. Gear ratio: 16.0:1-12.2:1. Overall ratio: 21.7:1-16.5:1. 3.2 turns lock to lock. 37-ft., 9-in. dia., curb to curb.

PERFORMANCE ... Quarter-mile (best): 14.49 sec., 93 mph

DIMENSIONS ... Wheelbase: 114.0-in.; front track: 60.0-in.; rear track: 60.0-in.; overall height: 54.4-in.; overall width: 77.2-in.; overall length: 199.0-in.; shipping weight: 3,650 lbs.; test weight: 3,905 lbs.; body/frame construction: unitized; fuel tank capacity: 21.5 gal. (19.5 Calif. cars).

EARTH MOVER

STEVE KELLY
Hot Rod, May 1970

The past is gone. The future may never see a car like this. It is one of the brutes, and all it needs is a way of staying in contact with terra firma.

HOT ROD ROAD TEST

That first supercar Chevelle, back in 1965, was some kind of a strong machine. It had a 375-horse 369, and while it lacked a few of the refinements that occur with aging, it began life as the hottest Chevrolet, except for Corvettes, ever to run off the end of an assembly line. The 350-horsepower 327 V-8 Chevy II was a fair equal, but the lengths to which it could be taken weren't as far-reaching as the inaugural issue of the SS396. The first model was a brute, and the last model of the Chevelle muscle car is the epitome of parts-gathering from existing bins for adapting to something that can and will perform. And last in the line of supercar products by Chevrolet may well be this one: a 454-ci, 460-horsepower, V-8–driven SS Malibu.

It could be the last because, even though buyers might still be available after 1971, strict legislation concerning emission outputs, coupled with ascending insurance rates, will render this car—or this type of car—worthless. Nonleaded gasoline will be mandatory in California late in 1971, and one year later the entire United States will follow. Unless some other way of using this kind of fuel is found, compression ratios of 8.5 to 9.0:1 will be the order of engine operation. When insurance rates reach one-third of a car's value, and that's the direction in which they're headed, it is usually not economically feasible to own this kind of thrasher. We savored every moment of this car, for the memory may have to last a long time. I hope this experience can be related well enough for all us to enjoy.

This particular Malibu is a hard one to trace through normal specification sheets and pricing literature. In a sense, it doesn't exist. Chevrolet doesn't emphasize that an LS6 454-ci V-8 option is available in anything other than a Corvette. But Chevelles can have it too, along with a cowl induction hood ($147.75), M-22 Muncie four-speed close-ratio gearbox ($221.90), and a limited-slip-equipment 4.10:1 rear axle ($25.30, special order). That's just some of the equipment our earth mover came with, plus the SS package that retails for $503. The LS6 is an additional $236.00, and although it shows as 450-horse when applied to Chevelle models, everything about it is identical to the 460. Chevrolet offers another 454-inch option, the LS5 engine (or Z15 option), and it is rated at 360 horsepower, but here again is an identical powerplant to the 390-horse variety fitted to big Chevys. The LS5 has a hydraulic lifter valve train, a one point lower compression (10.25:1), a Quadra-jet carburetor, a lower price, and a less startling performance. The $263 price difference is less than building up a 360/390- to a 450/460-horse version.

The M-22 Munice transmission is perfectly suited to this engine, but its linkage isn't. This one was probably the smoothest we've had, but the stick angle is such that it is easier to go from third to second than from third to fourth. All of us were leery of pulling the stick hard because the top mast is angled toward the driver, and unless he consciously pulls straight rearward, chances are good of the shifter catching on the neutral gate. It never went to second, except during low-speed tryouts to get the knack. The close-ratio box is noisy, and it has finer clutch drive gear splines than the regular production option M-22, as well as larger and heavier mainshaft rear splines and a pressed-on speedo drive gear. It is not directly interchangeable with the RPO M-22. Its heavier construction ensures a greater amount of reliability.

The front end isn't very aerodynamic, but it makes the grade on looks. A high view is splendid for today's muscle cars, but tomorrow will be different.

The best quarter-mile time was accomplished at Irwindale Raceway by John Dianna, who has a definite knack for this sort of thing. His low time of 13.44 seconds was followed by two other runs of 13.48 and 13.52, showing a consistent pattern. Shift points proved best at 6,100-6,200 rpm, and the maximum engine speed for coming off the line was 900 rpm. After some shock changes, the initial engine speed still couldn't be higher than 900, which is idle speed. There is so much bottom end on this car that it is impossible to use all of it effectively with street tires. These happened to be F70-14 Firestone Wide Ovals, with best pressure settings at 30 psi on the left rear and 28 psi on the right. Any throttle stabbing off the line would cause the tires to go up in smoke, and the car generally wanted to get sideways as a result. A decent set of drag slicks would naturally get more bite to the ground, but the immense amount of torque going through the drive line would just as naturally start breaking parts. Better to cool it and not have to walk home.

If this were our car, we'd invest in a big 9 3/4-inch ring gear carrier and housing, with a good traction bar setup. Traction bars are a good recommendation for stock rear setups. The 10.5-inch-diameter, bent-finger, single-disc clutch didn't even hint at giving up, even after 30 runs. We did get rid of some of the disc facing, increasing free-broad length, but that's merely an adjustment job. The pilot bearing got a little noisy after many back-to-back runs, and while an owner of such a car as this has the gearbox out to install

There's been some good planning on the inside. It's comfortable, and the panel arrangement is the best Chevy has ever done in this series. A thicker wheel rim and straighter shift level are needed. Add an oil gauge and the system would be great.

The back view kind of reminds us of a GTO, and that's a compliment. The dark section in rear bumper is a shock-absorbing, synthetic-material filler. Rear fender clearance is adequate for stock-class slicks and wide wheels.

a formidable scattershield, it will pay him to replace the throwout if the car has already logged a few thousand miles. This installation of a blast shield is mandatory for this car. Don't even think about not doing it. Chevrolet would've been smart in doing it on the line. Ours received a Lakewood shield.

Our better quarter-mile times were made when the air-filter element was removed and the engine was fairly warm, just a shade under the 195 degree mark. The warm motor killed a bit of the bottom end, making it easier to get the car moving. After a full cool-down, low-end torque was so tremendous that there was no way that the car would leave smoothly. It either bogged or it cranked the rear wheels into the outer limits. Torque isn't a passing phase in this 454. No matter what the shift point, the rear tires always spun off a bit of elapsed time with each upshift.

We can't vouch for the effectiveness of the cowl induction air inlet, but it seems that it would work better if it were both wider and farther to the rear. A plenum chamber using the domed selection of the hood and fed from an opening very near to the windshield offers more force-feeding action. The opening and closing action of the present door is actuated by a manifold vacuum.

If you can afford this car, you also have to feed its appetite, and this might result in a cost equal to monthly payments. An 11:25:1 compression ratio demands the best of leaded gasoline. Our poorest mileage figure was 7.30 miles per gallon and the best was 10.006. The average consumption turned out at 8.414. A full tank of fuel won't last 200 miles at this rate. And this 4150 series Holley was lean on the primary side, which has to be done to make engines like this pass emission tests. The lean condition causes minor surging in 60–70 mile-per-hour traffic.

Driving for the fun of it is a pleasant pastime. The 454 operates smoothly in congested traffic, and its handling is as good as other GM intermediates. We changed shock absorbers, adding Hurst/Gabriel Dual-Duty units. The stock Delco shocks have a 1.00-inch-diameter piston, and they really don't offer any drawbacks. The Hurst/Gabriels, with their 1-3/16-inch piston, combined with other refinements, simply made handling better. Power front disc/rear drum brakes are a part of the SS option, and so are the seven-inch-wide wheels. The variable ratio power steering and front and rear stabilizer bars, worked in with everything else, contributed to an overall good handler and a pleasant and very predictable road and highway car.

It's a quiet car too, even with the windows rolled down. Road and operational noise is well isolated. The interior treatment shows signs of approaching GTO and Olds 442 in both sophistication and quality. The optional instruments require $84.30 extra investment, but you can see them all and they all work. An oil pressure light is used, and there should be a pressure gauge available, working in conjunction with the warning light.

There are a lot more things we liked about this car than we found not to our liking. It's obvious the SS Malibu 454/450 isn't meant for paper routes or drivers who don't like being able to go quick and corner flat. An expensive proposition is what it is, and speed costs money, so it's a matter of how fast you care to go. It isn't charitable to throw stones at a dying breed, and while we all hope this isn't going to be the case, we'll just keep our five smooth stones waiting for some Goliath that says it can do as well, then doesn't.

CHEVELLE MALIBU SPORT COUPE 454

PRICE ... Base, $2,809.00; as tested, $4,852.30

ENGINE ... 454-ci OHC V-8, 4.251-in. bore x 4.00-in. stoke. 450 hp @ 5,600 rpm; 500 lbs.-ft. torque @ 3,600 rpm. 11.25:1 compression ratio. Bore spacing, 4.84-in.

CARBURETION ... Single Holley 4-barrel, 1.689-in. primary & secondary bores

VALVE TRAIN ... Solid lifters, .020-in. clearance intake & exhaust. 1.70:1 rocker ratio. Intake valve diameter, 2.190-in; exhaust, 1.880-in. Intake opens 62° BTC, closes 105° ABC, 347° duration. Exhaust opens 106° BBC, closes 73° ATC, 359° duration. Overlap, 135°. Alloy steel valves, aluminized face & head

DRIVE TRAIN ... Muncie M-22 4-speed. Ratios: 1st, 2.20:1; 2nd, 1:64:1; 3rd, 1.27:1; 4th, 1.0:1. 4.11:1 rear axle gear with limited-slip. 8.875-in.-dia. ring gear

BRAKES ... Front floating caliper disc/ rear drum with intergral vacuum assist. 11.0-in.-dia. disc, 9.5-in.-dia. drum.106.1-sq.-in. effective lining area

WHEELS & TIRES ... 14-in. X 7-in. steel wheels. F70-14 Firestones fiberglass bias-belted tires

SUSPENSION ... Front: Independent, short-long-arm type with coil spring & spherically jointed steering knuckle for each wheel. Double-acting tube shocks, 1.00-in. piston dia. Link-type stabilizer, .812-in.-dia. Rear: Salisbury axle with locations by upper and lower control arms. Coil springs and 1.00-in.-piston-dia. tube shocks

STEERING ... Power-assisted variable ratio. Semireversible, recirculating ball nut. Gear ratio: 16.1-12.4:1; overall ratio 18.7-12.4:1; 2.9 turns lock to lock, 16.25x15.50-in. wheel 42.5 ft. curb to curb turning dia.

PERFORMANCE ... Quarter-mile (best): 13.44 sec., 108.17 mph

DIMENSIONS ... Wheelbase: 112.0-in.; front track: 60.0-in.; rear track: 59.8-in.; overall height: 52.6-in.; overall width: 75.4-in.; overall length: 197.2-in.; shipping weight: 3,759 lbs.; body/frame construction; fuel tank capacity: 20 gal.

BEWARE THE QUIET FISH

STEVE KELLY
Hot Rod, January 1971

The 'Cuda 340 is the kind of car a person could like. It runs low-14 without breathing hard, takes corners without yelling and is big enough to be seen

Plymouth's Barracuda is offered in many configurations, but there's one that is best of all: the 'Cuda 340. What this car does is deliver a no-compromise performance exhibition at all stages, be it handling, drag racing, street riding, or cross-country junketing. Not many cars will do all of this well, although most cars can do them all to a certain degree. The 'Cuda 340 is not the ultimate weapon for Trans-Am racing unless properly prepared and placed in the hands of someone like Swede Savage. But it does beat a stock Z/28 or Boss 302 (at least the ones we've tested) through a quarter-mile. Because of the fair amount of lead the 340 would gain on a straightaway, it should be able to keep the aforementioned pair at bay long enough to still finish first over a fair-sized stretch of road-racing course.

This year's 'Cuda 340 has been given most of last year's AAR 'Cuda suspension pieces, but there are still a few tricks left that can only be had with extra money. These include quick steering and larger front disc/rear drum brakes, but from what this car told us, only the very serious corner bender need apply. The 'Cuda 340 is a far better-driving machine than either the 440 or 426 V-8–equipped 'Cudas, and at least equals the performance you might expect from an assembly-line-stock hemi 'Cuda. Both of the larger engines cost several hundred dollars more, weight is greater, and the cost of operating is a little harder to live with than with the 340. An odd thing that goes in favor of the 'Cuda 340 handling is that it depreciates overall car weight by 100 pounds when compared to the stock 383 V-8 (standard engine) 'Cuda. Only the 383 and the 340 'Cuda are fitted with rear stabilizers, which does much to get them around a curve first. The 440 six-barrel engine will easily run away from a 340 'Cuda, but not enough so for it to be an easy contest. A 'Cuda 340 is such an appealing supercar that it demands comparison to its foes.

This is still a supercar, not a medium-sized "compact" coupe. Insurance companies and drag racing sanctioning bodies have all figured out that the 275 horsepower is either a lot more honest than most car companies will issue, or a lot less. NHRA refactored the

A passing trio inspected the 'Cuda but were noncommital about its attraction for them. Plymouth has gone to four headlights on all '71 Barracudas.

rating several years ago, to somewhere in the 325 region, yet this hasn't hurt its competitiveness. When the 340 Chrysler was first introduced in 1968, it had almost the same equipment that is still featured. Alterations have been done to make it a cleaner engine, and the '71 version has a Carter Thermo·Quad carburetor. The Carter AVS four-barrel fitted originally had 1.44-inch-diameter primary bores and 1.69-inch-diameter secondaries. The T·Q now used has smaller primaries (1.38 inches), with huge secondaries (2.25 inches). It sure helps. It helps lower emission readings, especially at low engine speed, and keeps the top end running better when the demand is high. It is also a good ice-breaker for Carter, and because it is now an original-equipment item, the price of the Thermo·Quad may go down. Other than carburetion, the '71 340 engine is like it was in '68.

Standard transmission on the 340 'Cuda is a three-speed, but an automatic or four-speed should be ordered. The TorqueFlite on 340 cars has a specific valve plate to push shift points up near 6,000 rpm. There are gobs of torque buried in this engine, and the four-speed takes advantage of it better than the automatic. Our 'Cuda had a four-speed and 3.55:1 limited-slip rear end. It got better times when short-shifted, though it never did go slow.

There were nearly 1,500 miles on the clock by the time we took it to Lions Drag Strip for an afternoon of thrashing, and its first run came only minutes after John Dianna drove it through the gate. The trunk was emptied for the ultimate in drag-strip prepara-

The dash panel is shaped like those in big Plymouths. The cluster in front of the driver contains every gauge or control. All are easy to find. Vent controls are center-mounted, and air inlet control for hood scoop is there, too.

tion. Johnny then banged out a 14.53-second elapsed time, with a speed of 98.57 miles per hour. The next trip was worth 14.41 seconds and 99.44 miles per hour. The air cleaner element was removed and the engine cooled, and within four more runs, the 'Cuda had dropped to 14.18 seconds. From this point on, it got stuck in a top-end groove. No matter what the elapsed time, it ran either 100.22 or 100.33 miles per hour. Couldn't break away, no matter how we tried. The Pure Stock record at Lions for the 'Cuda 340 class is 14.09 and a speed of 99 miles per hour. At least we beat one end of the record. Had we gone deeper, say to the point of timing or tire pressure experimentation, we would've bettered both marks. A Dart 340 tested in 1968 ran 14.38 with an automatic, and a Duster 340 with a very sick transmission/clutch assembly in 1970 stayed in the 15-second class. Compared to other makes, this 'Cuda beat the '69 Z/28, which ran 14.34 with 4.56:1 rear gear, and the '70 Boss 302, which recorded a 14.62 elapsed time. Both of them weighed less than the 'Cuda, so if you care to discuss potential, I think it's obvious which car shows the most. Do you still want a discussion?

It didn't take us long to find out the best shifting pattern. Chrysler Corporation four-speeds are notoriously evil from gear to gear because the gears themselves are so large it's hard to get the synchros lined up quickly enough to make consistent power shifts. The higher the engine speed, the more time needed to synchronize (i.e., slow down) the next gear. Dianna began short-shifting the car on his third run, which eventually resulted in sub-14.20-second times. Not only did this prove beneficial to quarter-mile times, but it put shift points closer to the peak torque curve. Had there been more rear wheelspin between first and second than there was, we would've lost time. We didn't, but a set of seven-inch Goodyear or Firestone slicks sure could've put us at or in the 13-second bracket. Original shift points were 6,000 rpm, and when we lowered them, 5,300 to 5,500 rpm was where the best times were earned. Short-shifting effected a temporary cure, but to further help the matter, a competition shifter might allow more consistent shifts without fear of gearbox damage. Even then, short-shifting will help stock-condition times.

When the engine is run up to six grand, and shifts are made, this usually imposes an

Hood pins and shaker scoop are extras. Unlike others, this scoop doesn't shake. It also doesn't block forward vision.

extra load on the drivetrain because second gear is contacted with such force it really shocks the driveshaft and rear end. Unless internal transmission reworking is done by a qualified soul, stick to early-shifting a quality shifter. One thing we all thought might not be too good, but one that drew no complaint, is the pistol-grip shifter. After using it, we have laid to rest premature objections.

If you've been reading us for the past year, you recall the project Duster story that had a full report in June 1970. The stock, base-line car with its gearbox malady didn't do too well. But by the time our straight-line stocker expert got it all together, Johnny's

With firm suspension, the 'Cuda doesn't lift the front end much when leaving the line. But the horsepower does get back to the rear end, as witnessed by our good elapsed times. High-rate leaf springs and good mounting prevent wheel hop.

Duster ran a best elapsed time of 11.41, against a C/Modified Production record (at the time) of 11.45 seconds. This project has resulted in perhaps the largest number of inquiries regarding *Hot Rod* project cars since we got involved in this kind of work. Because of its impressive performance, Dianna has taken the car to his bosom and will campaign it throughout the '71 season in the lower M/P classes. Duster and Demon bodies are lighter than a Barracuda by more than 200 pounds, and when one of our "drag racing" sister PPC competitors put a 340 Demon into test car service, we looked for it to run quicker than our 340 'Cuda. But it didn't, for some reason. Presently, that car's best elapsed time has been in the 14.50s, which is still respectable, but maybe it needs some short-shifting. Maybe it just means a 'Cuda works better.

The 'Cuda 340 isn't all work and no play. It is a good road car, yet the rear suspension is stiffer than on the Z/28 and Boss 302, so wide tar strips and quick bumps are felt more in the 'Cuda. After a week's possession the car, however, we didn't notice this.

Steering is good, with only a hint of understeer. The rear bar and fat tires induce some oversteer to the car's angle of twisting around bends, so a driver never feels as if he's sliding his front wheels where they're not expected to go. Successive hard stops

Wide-tread Goodyear GTs measure eight inches across contact surface and do really good things for handling. Stylists must keep busy from year to year, so now there are fender louvers where none were before.

Taking out filter element helped times a bit. The fresh-air scoop is really fastened down well. The engine runs relatively cool and most parts are easy to reach.

don't do a thing to the brakes except warm them up, after which they work better than when they are relatively cool.

The interior of the 'Cuda is large. It seems way too big for such a small car, but then it is. As front seat passengers, we were never cramped for space in any direction. As for the rear seat, it's large for a sporty car, but that doesn't mean I'd volunteer to spend a week there.

Chrysler Corporation has evidently taken steps to improve body quality. This production-line car didn't leak air or water. Wide doors with large side glass probably aren't the easiest assemblies to install, and the ones on this car were wont to shake when rolled down or when the doors were shut. Barracudas of all shapes and sizes are now in a declining part of a new car market. This is too bad, but it is fact. Despite the fact that there are fewer people buying this kind of car now than two years ago, there's no apology required from this car's manufacturer for it being the fault of the product. A 'Cuda 340 is a super supercar.

1971 'CUDA 340

PRICE … Base, $3,134.00; as tested, $3,971.00

ENGINE … 340-ci V-8, 275 horsepower @ 5,000 rpm, 340 lbs.-ft. torque @ 3,200 rpm, 10.5:1 compression ratio, drop-forged connecting rods and crankshaft, dual exhaust system

CARBURETION … Carter Thermo-Quad No. TQ4972S four-barrel, 1.38-inch-dia. primaries, 2.25-inch-dia. sec.

VALVE TRAIN … Hydraulic lifters, 1.5:1 rocker ratio. Intake opens 22° BTC, closes 66° ABC, 268° duration. Exhaust opens 74° BBC, closes 22° ATC, 276° duration; 44° overlap. Intake head diameter 2.02 in.; 1.60-in.-dia. exhaust

DRIVE TRAIN … All-synchro 4-speed. Ratios: 2.47 low, 1.7 second, 1.34 third, 1.0 fourth. 10.5-in.-dia. Borg & Beck finger-release clutch. Separable 8 3/4-in.-dia. ring gear differential, friction bias limited-slip, 3.55:1 ratio

BRAKES … Front disc, rear drum with power booster. 10.7-in.-dia. vented, cast-iron rotor; 10-in.-dia. rear drum. 138.1-sq.-in. effective lining area. Front to rear brake effectiveness: 60% front, 40% rear

WHEELS & TIRES … 15-x7-in. steel wheels; five 1/2-20 lugs on 4 1/2-in. circle. E60-15 Goodyear Wide Tread Polyglas tires

SUSPENSION … Front: Independent, lateral, nonparallel control arms with 111-lb.-per-inch (wheel rate) alloy steel torsion bars. Std. .94-inch stabilizer bar, tube shocks. Rear: Parallel, longitudinal leaf springs (57x2.5 in.), with 132 lb.-per-in. rating at wheel. Link-type rear stabilizer

STEERING … Chrysler integral power assist with recirculating ball; 15.7:1 gear ratio, 19.0:1 overall ratio. 3.5 turns lock to lock. 38.4 ft. curb to curb turning diameter. 16.0-in.-dia. wheel. Parallelogram equal-length tie rods

PERFORMANCE … Quarter-mile (best): 14.18 sec., 100.33 mph

DIMENSIONS … Wheelbase: 108 in.; front track: 59.7 in.; rear track: 60.7 in.; overall height: 51.2 in.; overall width: 74.9 in.; overall length: 186.6 in.; test weight: 3,620 lbs.; shipping weight: 3,565 lbs.; body/frame construction: unitized; fuel tank capacity: 18 gal.

PONTIAC'S ANSWER TO THE GTO

STEVE KELLY
Hot Rod, June 1971

Good thing Pontiac had the GTO in their pocket; it made it easier to come up with a mild-mannered successor. They call it the GT-37. We call it high performance on a low-lead diet

Pontiac's GT-37 is a rub-off from the GTO. This isn't accidental. As the GTO got better, it got more expensive; and its image did nothing to reduce the insurance costs. While the GT-37 isn't the kind of car you can buy for nothing down and $20.00 a week for 36 months (what is?), it has a relatively reasonable price. Naturally, Pontiac wishes to have those who'd buy a GTO, if it weren't for the expense, choose the GT-37. It looks something like a GTO but is lightly equipped in basic form. Rubber floor covering is the first tip-off, but I really didn't notice this until some time after picking up the car. It just doesn't make that much difference.

The GT-37 is actually a T-37 series "Tempest" with a GT option, and this includes an abundance of dress-up items, with the only driveline boost a heavy-duty three-speed transmission. The striping over the wheel-opening flares sets the car off nicely, but as we found out after having an errant driver ding one fender, you just can't go to the parts counter for replacement tape stripes. When we ordered the car, it was requested with a 350 four-barrel V-8. Alas, Pontiac no longer offers one, so we settled for a 400 Quadrajet-carbureted engine. It also carried a four-speed (wide-ratio), and the axle ratio turned out to be 3.55:1. Pontiac offers an assembly-line-installed 3.90:1 rear gear, but someone who takes care of car ordering in Michigan isn't aware of how much better one of their cars will turn the quarter with a 3.90. Better the 3.55 than a 3.23, which is also offered. With the 400 engine and the four-speed, our metallic blue GT-37 falls in the supercar category, meaning that it is assessed a penalty by underwriters. Sorry. A 455 four-barrel engine, either conventionally equipped or built for high output, can be ordered in this model, and you can imagine what the guy at the insurance office would say about this. One other thing this car could've had, but didn't, is a close-ratio M-22 (2.20:1 low) coarse-pitch-gear Muncie four-speed. As it turned out, we didn't need it, and the wide-ratio (2.52:1 low gear) transmission may have been better in that it provided better low-end torque to the rear wheels. The production Hurst shifter was in sad shape when we first

The GT-37 option includes nameplates, stripes, and hood pins. The front body panel is a compression-molded, fiberglass/plastic sheet.

picked up the car, but a talented mechanic at Los Angeles' Farrar-Bach Pontiac dealership really put it back together better than we could believe.

After making sure everything was "in spec" on the GT-37, we took it to Orange County International Raceway for a day of tripping the light beams. While a 400-ci engine offers an abundance of torque, horsepower (and torque) are hurt when compression is restricted to a maximum of 8.2:1. We really weren't expecting much for quarter-mile times. The clutch seemed to be wearing thin, so after adjusting it almost to the end of the throwout adjustment rod, we took it over the O.C.I.R. asphalt, shifting at 5,000 rpm. This netted a 14.565-second elapsed time and a speed of 96.87 miles per hour. This is surprising, though not unbelievable. On the second run, we put the needle a little higher on the tach before leaving and lost .13-second and 1.23 miles per hour. Varying the shift points to speeds under 5,000 didn't help, and going higher had no effect. The '71 model four-barrel 400 and 455 engine air cleaners have larger air-inlet capacities than their '71 counterparts, so taking the air cleaner off altogether obviously will get more air to the Quadrajet. A change has also been made to the secondary throttle opening

Since most intermediate Pontiacs are designed for lots of accessories, the absence of them leaves a fantastic amount of working space around the engine.

on this year's Pontiac four-barrel Rochesters. Whereas the earlier units took a maximum of two and a half seconds to open, the '71 carbs take only one second. They feel better during the transition stage now, thanks to a lessening of time for "stumble" to occur.

Removing the large air filter and shifting the car at 5,000 rpm showed the filter removal was worth a .05-second elapsed time improvement (14.51), and the speed went up to 97.29 miles per hour. Looks as though the filter unit causes a little top-end asthma, though we wouldn't run a car on the street without one. In most cases, it is unlawful to do so. The best recorded run with the car breathing better was a 14.40-second time with a speed of 97.50 miles per hour. During this run we shifted from first and second at 5,000, but held third to 5,400. Far as we can tell, nothing else was different. Incidentally, viewing both the optional dash-mounted tachometer and the fuel gauge is made difficult

A thick-rimmed Formula wheel carries our highest recommendation, even though it partially hides the tach and fuel gauge. A round speedometer sure has it over horizontal meters as far as ease of seeing and reading goes.

The GT-37 leaves the line without any trace of wheel hop, and because the Quadrajet now opens its secondary system quicker, there is little chance of stumble through the transition stage on acceleration.

by the addition of the extra-cost ($58) Formula steering wheel. We'd hate to have such a car (or any car) without this kind of tiller, so maybe it is better to forsake ordering the factory tach and install a more visible accessory unit later. According to an Edmunds' New Car Prices book, the instrument option can be ordered without the tachometer, and the direct reading gauges make it.

After doing drag strip examinations for the GT-37, we thought a turn around Orange County's road circuit was in order, especially since this Pontiac had sturdy underpinnings. After negotiating the "hard" parts, we began slowing down along a straight section, but when the clutch was depressed, to downshift from fourth to third, the pedal hung against the floor. That bit about being nearly to the end of the adjustment had meant that something important *could* happen. Fortunately we weren't in a highly precarious part of the track and did manage to slow it down and coast to the pits. As this is written, the dealer who is dismantling the clutch assembly hasn't told us what the problem was on the 10.4-inch-diameter semicentrifugal (bent-finger) clutch. Maybe it wasn't the clutch. While pushing the pedal activated the throwout arm, it could've been an internal rupture on the arm or possibly the throwout bearing. We'll know later.

1971 PONTIAC GT-37

PRICE ... Base, $2,807.00; as tested, $4,331.80

ENGINE ... 400-ci V-8, 300 horsepower @ 4,800 rpm, 400 lbs.-ft. torque @ 3,600 rpm. 8.2:1 compression ratio. 4.12-in bore x 3.745-in. stroke

CARBURETION ... Rochester Quadrajet 4-barrel 1.38-in.-dia. primary bores, 2.25-in. secondary

VALVE TRAIN ... Hydraulic lifters. 2.11-in-dia. intake; 1.77-in.-dia. exhaust. Timing: Intake opens 23° BTC, closes 70° ATC, duration 2/3°; exhaust opens 78° BBC, closes 31° ATC; duration: 289°. Lift at valve: .410-in. intake, .413-in. exhaust. Valve overlap: 54°. Camshaft parts number: 9779067

DRIVE TRAIN ... 4-speed wide-ratio transmission. 2.52:1 low, 1.88:1 2nd, 1.46:1 3rd, 1.00:1 4th. Fully synchronous. Bent-finger-type semicentrifugal 10.4-in.-dia. clutch. 3.55-to-1 ratio axle, 8.125-inch ring gear

BRAKES ... Front disc/rear drum with power assist. 10.94-in.-o.d. rotor, 9.5-in. cast-iron drum. 103.6-sq.-in. effective lining area. 62.6% front to rear effectiveness

WHEELS & TIRES ... Steel "honeycomb" 14-in. x 6-in. wheels. G70-14 Performa GT B.F. Goodrich bias-belted tire

SUSPENSION ... Front: Independent with upper & lower control arms. .937-in.-dia. link-type stabilizer, 1.0-in.-dia. piston tube shocks, 335 lb.-per-in. rate coil springs. Rear: One-piece housing with four-link pivoted control arms. 1.0-in. piston dia. tube shocks. 200 lb.-per-in. rate coil springs

STEERING ... Variable-ratio Saginaw power, coaxial linkage, recirculating ball bearing. Overall ratio: 18.9 to 15.3:1. Gear ratio: 16.0:1 to 13.0:1. 3.5 turns lock to lock, 37.4-ft. curb-to-curb turning dia.

PERFORMANCE ... Quarter-mile (best): 14.40 sec., 97.50 mph

DIMENSIONS ... Wheelbase: 112.0 in.; front track: 61.0 in.; rear track: 60.0 in.; overall height: 52.0 in.; overall width: 76.7 in.; overall length: 202.8 in.; test weight: 3,675 lbs.; shipping weight: N/A; body/frame construction: separate frame; fuel tank capacity: 19 gal.

Driveability of the GT-37 on city streets is something like the early Road Runner ('68-'69) in terms of ride. Most GM "performance" cars have a smooth street ride because of their coil spring suspension, and if they handle well it is because front and rear stabilizers are used. The GTO is one example of this. But the GT-37 doesn't have a rear bar, so to make it handle, it has been fitted with fairly high-rate springs. This makes riding harsh when compared to a GTO, but it does assist handling. Even with the stiff springs, it does understeer during an "all-out" cornering maneuver, which points out the reason for a rear stabilizer bar. There'd be no great difficulty adapting a GTO shaft to a GT-37. It's a bolt-on.

A peculiar aspect of the GT-37 is that when you're driving it, especially at freeway speeds, you're unaware of the car itself. This is a plus factor. Instead of having to accustom himself to odd controls, difficult wheel position, poor visibility, or uncomfortable seating, the driver is comfortable and able to concentrate on just driving. It's the kind of car that makes you feel welcome.

The Pontiac honeycomb wheel looks like aluminum yet is all-steel with a urethane coating on center section only.

Among the GT-37 trick option parts is dual-dual exhaust tips. Does this have anything to do with a new Pontiac secret?

Driveability of the GT-37 on city streets tested similar to the early Road Runner (1968–69) in terms of ride.

INDEX

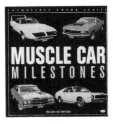

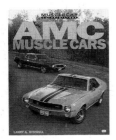

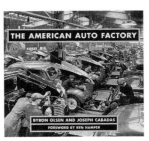